Pendle Hill and its Coven of 13 Moors

A guided walk in the heart of Pendle Witch country

by

PETER G. CLARKE

About the route

Historically, Pendle Hill and its surrounding inhabitants were immersed in the real life Witch trials of 1612 and the extensive folklore that followed. As recent as 2012, just before the 400th anniversary of the Pendle Witch trials, engineers working for United Utilities on the maintenance of the Lower Black Moss reservoir dam, unearthed the remains of a 17th century cottage along with a cat that had been entombed in its walls. Archeologists confirmed the age of the cottage and that opened up a discussion with Historians as to whether or not this could have been the long lost Malkin Tower, the dwelling place of Elizabeth Southerns (known as Demdike), and where the Witches Coven last met on Good Friday 1612. Even if Historians can't agree on whether or not it was Malkin Tower, its find, so close to the anniversary, will certainly add further to the folklore. The cottage was found near to the Hamlet of Overhouses, which, by the way, we pass through on section 2 of the walk.

Across Europe, a Coven is recognised as a gathering of 13 Witches, and it's therefore fitting that Pendle Hill happens to have thirteen moors gathered around it, all of which we will visit on the walk.

The thirteen moors clockwise from the 'Nick O Pendle' are: Pendleton, Mearley, Pendle, Worston, Downham, Barley, Ing Head, Annel Cross, Twiston, Rimington, Stang Top, Spence and Wiswell.

The hill is also directly linked to the Quaker Movement, through its founder George Fox, who climbed the hill in 1652, whereupon he had a vision that went on to inspire the followers of the movement. There is a plaque recording this near the summit shelter.

The walk is divided into three sections, between 4–7 miles each, making a total distance of 17.1 miles, with a height gain of 3,260 ft. The maximum elevation is Pendle Hill trig point at 1,827 ft.

The route can be walked as a whole or in sections, and offers something for everyone.

The challenge of a 17 mile walk, a walk steeped in not only gradient, but also rich in local history and folklore.

The guide, graphically brings together the extensive views from the moorland plateau, the varied guide/boundary stones and stiles (both new and old), Trig points, summits, stories and a mix of fact, folklore and legend.

As you traverse the moors you can be confident that you will be immersing yourself in the experience, that is, the 'Pendle Hill and its Coven of 13 Moors' walk.

Pendle Hill and its coven of 13 moors walk
is published by Peter G. Clarke

This edition published 2024

All text, Photographs, renderings, art media effects
and hand drawn maps are by the Author

978-1-3999-7706-7

1 3 5 7 9 10 8 6 4 2

Typeset by Falcon Oast Graphic Art Ltd, www.falcon.uk.com
Printed and bound in Great Britain by ImprintDigital.com

Contents

Acknowledgements v

Full route map vi

Introduction 1

Section 1 Nick o' Pendle (Clitheroe Rd) to Gate on Ing Head Moor (Barley Ln) 6

Section 2 Kissing gate Ing Head Moor (Barley Ln) on a roughly circular route back to Pendleside (Barley Ln) 42

Section 3 Pendleside (Barley Ln) to Nick o' Pendle crossover to Wiswell Moor Trig and back to Nick o' Pendle (Clitheroe Rd) 142

Index to the Guide 212

List of Maps to accompany the guide 216

Notes on sources of Information 217

Acknowledgements

Thanks to my Daughter in law, Dr. Katie Clarke for spurring me on to write the guide (see page 72)

To my wife Anne for prompting the 'Coven' link, thus adding to the local folklore, and for putting up with my long hours spent on the hill and moors recceing and photographing

And, to my middle son Russell for the invaluable critiquing and checking out the sections of the route, which, being a Harrier, he likes to run

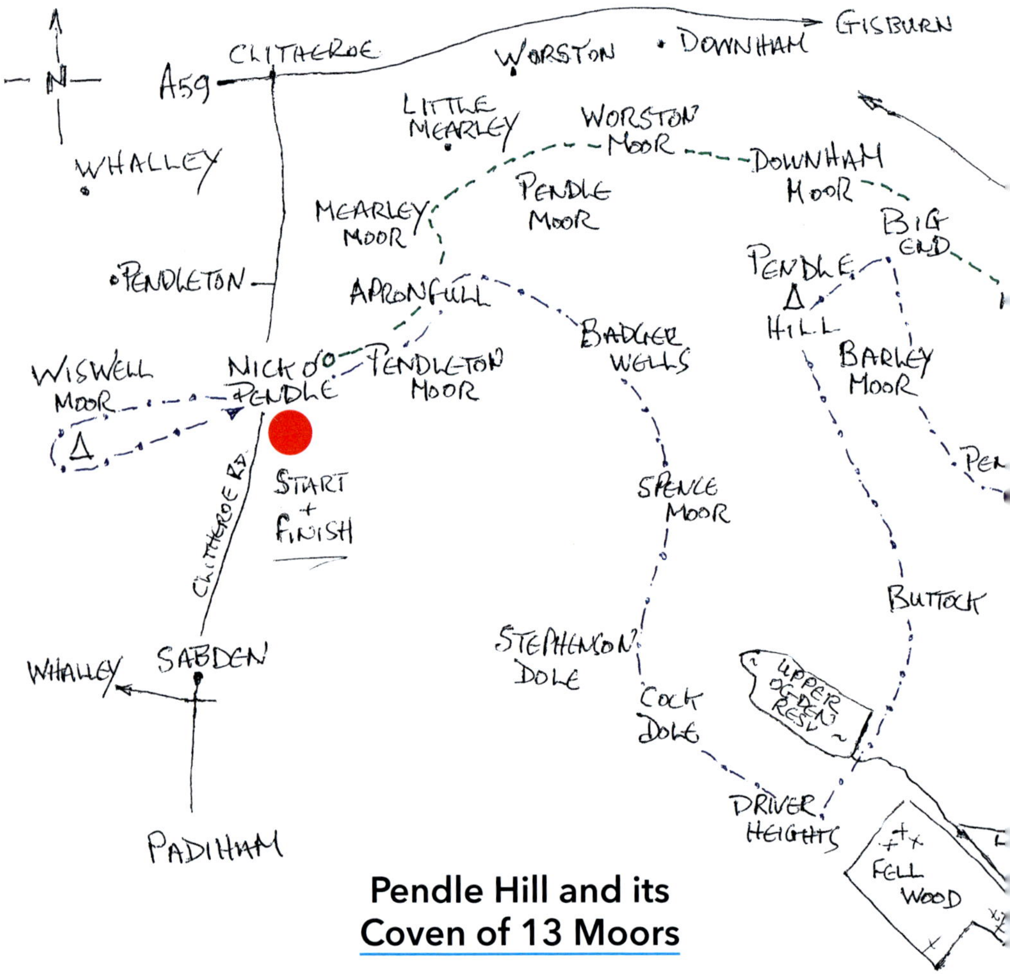

Pendle Hill and its Coven of 13 Moors

Overall route 17.1 miles

Ascent 3,260 ft

Maximum elevation – Pendle Hill
Trig point 1,827 ft

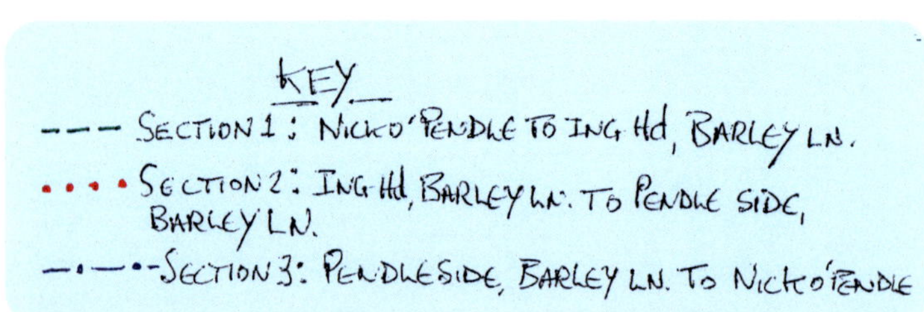

HIGHER TWISTON
SMITHY FOLD
LANE ENDS
COOLHAM FARM
OCCUPATION LANE
ANNEL CROSS MOOR
BLACKO
TWISTON MOOR
RIMINGTON MOOR
SALT PIE
FOUR LANE ENDS
WINDY HARBOUR
HELLIWELL WOOD
UPPER BLACK MOSS RESV
LOWER BLACK MOSS RESV
HIGHER BLACKMOSS
AITKEN WOOD AND SCULPTURE TRAIL
BARLEY
MOUNTAIN FARM
BLACKO
STANG TOP MOOR
STANG TOP
BARLEY VILLAGE AND PICNIC SITE
BLACKO
WHITE HOUGH
NARROWGATES
ROUGHLEE
NEWCHURCH-IN-PENDLE (WITCHES GALORE'S SHOP)

Introduction

The picturesque, circular walking route around Pendle Hill is made up of three sections, of between 4 - 7 miles each, with a combined total distance of 17.1 miles, and a height gain of 3,260 ft. Maximum elevation is Pendle Hill trig point at 1,827 ft.

The first of the three sections starts from the Nick o' Pendle in order to give the opportunity to take time out on section 2 at Barley picnic site (roughly half way round). Barley is the only place on the route with any facilities.

If you just wanted to do a shorter walk, then Section 2 (walking clockwise and starting and finishing at Barley Picnic site) would make a particularly nice six mile circular.

In order to get the best from the walk i.e. maximize the views, ease route finding and minimize the risks associated with being out in bad weather, it is recommended to do the walk on a fine, clear and settled day. The design of the guide, with hand drawn maps, pictures and text means that on a good day there should be no need to use a map or compass

Section 1 Nick o' Pendle (Clitheroe Rd) [Grid Ref.SD7725 386] to Ing Head Moor and kissing gate to (Barley Ln) [Grid Ref. SD814 418]

Section 2 Kissing gate Ing Head Moor (Barley Ln) [Grid Ref. SD814 418] on a circular route back to Pendleside (Barley Ln) [Grid Ref.SD8145 416]

Section 3 Pendleside (Barley Ln) [Grid Ref.SD8145 416] to Nick o' Pendle, crossover to Wiswell Moor Trig and back to the Nick o' Pendle (Clitheroe Rd), [Grid Ref.SD7725 386] ***and the finish***

Background Notes

In the guide I mention the following:

> A Track – generally meaning something that could also be used, in general, by off-road vehicles, tractors, ..
>
> A Path – generally meaning a well-worn and visible path
>
> A Trod – generally meaning a rough, often intermittent trail, infrequently used except for the odd, walker, runner or sheep
>
> (When following trods it's important to look ahead and keep moving in the general direction of your route, so that it does not matter if you lose the trail here and there. Trods are difficult for route finding, particularly in low visibility weather)

The route is generally good underfoot on the tops, but the low lying moors and fields, in particular, can be really boggy in bad weather, with some being poor all year round). In snowy conditions you could expect thigh deep drifts on the wind swept tops and in the Cloughs. Twiston and Rimington moors have areas with indistinct paths (more like sheep trods, as well as tussock grass, reeds and boggy sections). Spence moor is also very boggy on the ascent, so much so that it never seems to dry out. More specific detail is given in the introduction to each section of the guide.

Safety concerns

Apart from the occasional drystone wall, or ruins thereof, on the 2-3 square miles of high wind swept moors there are only two shelters, one on Pendle Moor and one at the Big End, and as the tops can be lashed by freezing winds, rain, and sleet, care must be taken to ensure you prepare very well according to the conditions. Specific equipment may be necessary on some occasions, for example: *Cold wintry weather – good quality slip on spikes for moving over frozen or iced ground, and sunglasses to prevent snow blindness on a snow covered sunny day. For a hot sunny day – sun block/cream and hat, and plenty of water*

The Hill can be regularly claggy, and with so many intersecting paths and trods as well as featureless tops and moors, route finding can be very difficult. As such you need to have, and be competent with, a map and compass. Wherever possible, walking on roads was kept to a minimum, but never the less we have the following:

> Two road crossing points – one at the Nick and another at Barley Ln
>
> Also there are two short (approx. 170yd each) road sections, at lower Black Moss and Stang Top
>
> And finally there is just over 1,200yds of road on Barley Lane, from the kissing gate at Ing Head moor past the four lane ends to the gate for Coolham Farm and Twiston Moor
>
> Although, the roads are small rural ones, there are blind bends and brows so caution must be exercised and always stay alert

Mobile phone signal is patchy and intermittent, and as such cannot be relied upon for communication or route finding

Dogs

It should be noted that all the moors are grazed by hill Sheep and Lambs, Deer and Hare as well as being home to Grouse, Pheasant, Lapwing, Curlew and other ground nesting birds so you must make sure you keep dogs on a lead at all times. Some dog owners have a bad habit of bagging the poo up, but then leaving the bag hung on a wall, fence or gate to which they never return

– and this, rightly so, causes unnecessary friction with locals, farmers and landowners.

Photos of all gates and stiles are shown in the guide, but it's best pointing out that some stiles are not big dog friendly

Gates, Fences, walls

Ensure gates are left as you find them, and do not climb the drystone walls or fences

Litter

Please minimize the impact on the environment, make sure you leave things as you found them, and taking your entire waste and recycling items home with you. ***All you should leave behind are your footprints, and take only memories***

Tourist/Visitor facilities

Barley village is well connected with scheduled bus services from Burnley, Nelson, Colne and Clitheroe.

Unless you take the option for a break on (Sect.2) at the 'Barley Picnic site', the route has no facilities, and as such you must ensure you are self-sufficient for the duration – particularly in terms of fluids

At time of writing Barley had the following: (Always check the current status & opening times before you set out)

> Barley Parish Council has paid car parking with free Toilet facilities. Always check opening times in advance, but at time of writing, hours of opening are – Oct-Mar 8am–6pm, and Apr-Sept 8am-9pm
>
> The 'Pendle Inn' and the 'Barley Mow' are both highly recommended for food and drink, and both offer

accommodation. Both are also dog friendly

'The Cabin' – Café & takeaway located in the car park

'Boothman Park' is close by, and offers a range of activities, as well as accommodation.

The village of Sabden which is off the route, had, at time of writing, the following: (Always check the current status & opening times before you set out)

Pub Restaurants

Café/Sandwiches

Post Office/store

Accommodation

2–300yds off route over the summit of the Nick on the Clitheroe side is the 'The Wellsprings' Pub, Restaurant and Café

Villages of Downham, and Worston **which are also off the route**, offer food, drink, and accommodation

Finally, on a really clear day the views are stunning and far reaching – *so don't forget your camera and binoculars!*

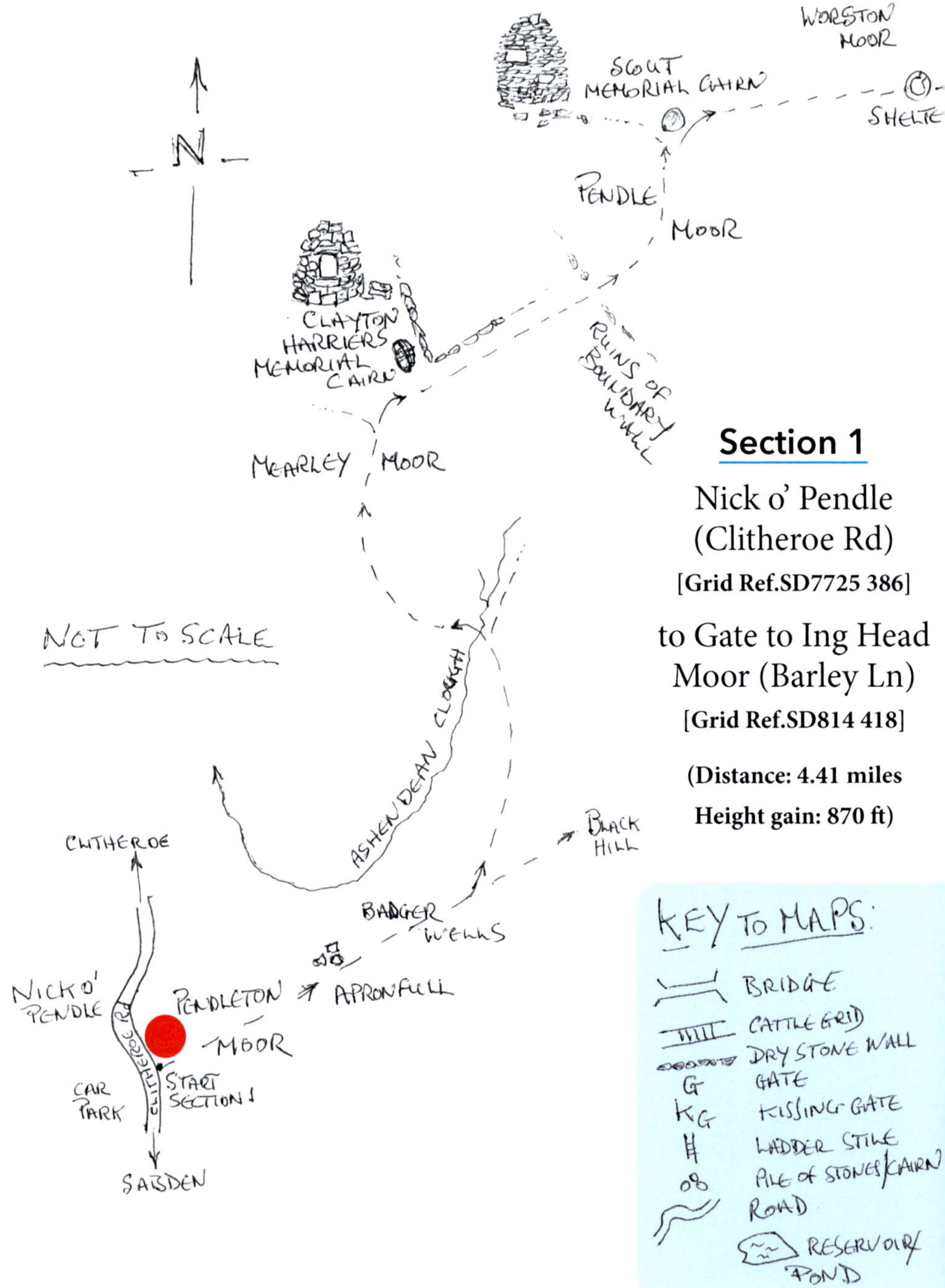

Section 1

Nick o' Pendle (Clitheroe Rd)

[Grid Ref.SD7725 386]

to Gate to Ing Head Moor (Barley Ln)

[Grid Ref.SD814 418]

(Distance: 4.41 miles

Height gain: 870 ft)

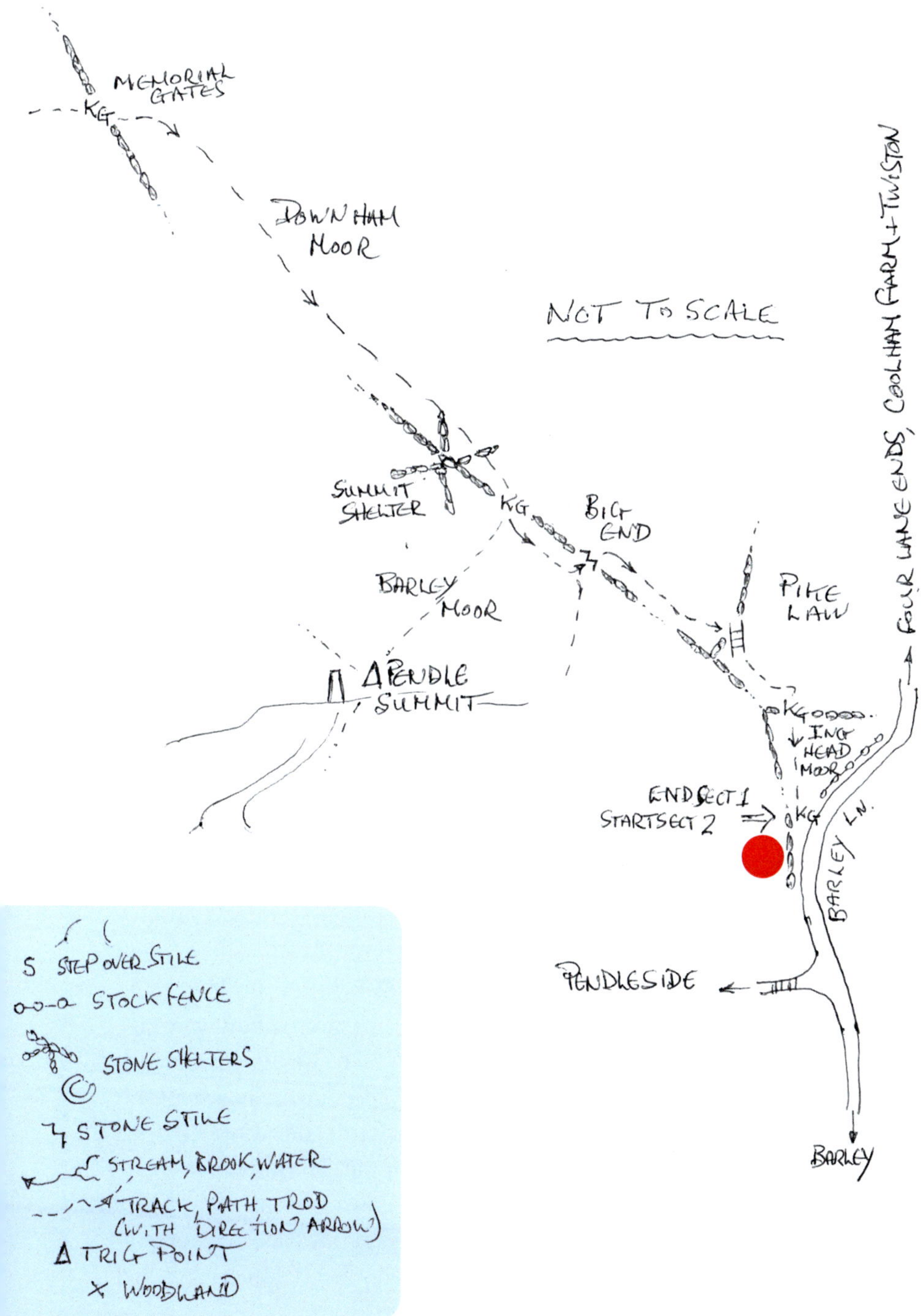
MEMORIAL GATES
KG
DOWNHAM MOOR
NOT TO SCALE
SUMMIT SHELTER
KG
BIG END
BARLEY MOOR
PIKE LAW
PENDLE SUMMIT
FOUR LANE ENDS, COOLHAM FARM + TWISTON
KG
ING HEAD MOOR
END SECT 1
START SECT 2
KG
BARLEY LN.
PENDLESIDE
BARLEY
STEP OVER STILE
STOCK FENCE
STONE SHELTERS
STONE STILE
STREAM, BROOK, WATER
TRACK, PATH, TROD (WITH DIRECTION ARROW)
TRIG POINT
WOODLAND

1.1 Summit of Nick o' Pendle (Clitheroe Rd) from Sabden side. Wiswell Moor is off to the left and the route over Pendleton Moor is off to the right.

On a Historical note Pendleton Moor and Apronfull were used in 1842 for a Rally by a 2,500 strong group of the 'Chartists Working Class Movement' which was founded to lobby for workers rights. Such a thing was seen as a threat to the establishment and quite often rallies would be dispersed by Cavalry, and sometimes Infantry, from the local Barracks in the Mill town of Burnley. Built in 1820, the Barracks were originally for Cavalry, and later Infantry, until closure in 1898. Having been a Barracks Town, Burnley provided 3-4,000 soldiers for WW1. Initially, the soldiers were based in the French town of Fécamp where the 'Bénédictine' liquer was made, and this quickly became their favourite tipple. To this day, the 'Burnley Miners club' is the World's no.1 consumer of what is locally called 'Benny'. The drink is often mixed with hot water to make a 'Benny & Hot'. It's also served at the Burnley FC (Clarets) matches.

1.2 There is ample off-road parking at the top of the Nick in the disused Quarry areas on the Sabden side. There is also a tarmacked parking area just over the cattle grid on the left on the way down to Sabden.

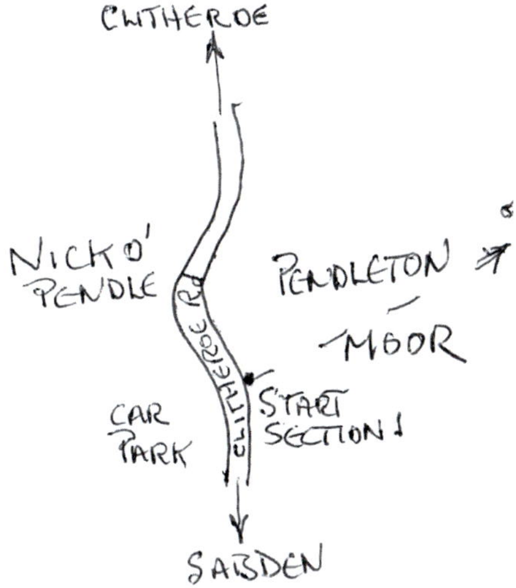

1.3 The Memorial to the Airman who crashed in bad weather nearby during WW2.

1942 F/Sgt Goulter (AAF) was tranferring his 'Boulton Paul Defiant Turret' fighter plane from Manby to Walney Island, near Barrow, when he was hit by a very severe hailstorm, which resulted in him crashing near Gisburn.

1944 US airmen were flying five P47D 'Thunderbolts' from East Wretham in Norfolk to RAF Warton, near Preston, in low visibility weather, and against advice. The weather worsened dramatically as the flight got closer to the destination, and unfortunately one of them crashed whilst attempting to land at RAF Warton, and it's thought that a second one piloted by F/O Runnells, was circling above in hope of clearing weather, but ran out of fuel and crashed into the side of Mearley.

About this section

Starting from the Nick, this section takes in seven of the thirteen moors (Pendleton, Mearley, Pendle, Worston, Downham, Barley and Ing Head) on a steady ascent across the moorland plateau towards the big end, with the steepest part of the ascent being the initial climb up on to Apronfull.

It's generally good going underfoot at the start, then becoming boggy on the side of Ashendean Clough and both Mearley & Pendle moors

On a clear day, as you cross Pendleton, Mearley and Pendle moors you get great views of some of the Villages and Hamlets on the Northern and Western sides of Pendle as well as Longridge, Beacon and Bowland Fells and the Coast.

Further away you get to see some of the Yorkshire Dales Peaks and on a really clear day the South Lakeland peaks

With the views on this section being mainly to the South West, West and North West it makes it good for photos as the morning sun is behind you.

1.4 View of start looking north east from Nick across Pendleton moor to Apronfull

The route starts from the Nick trending north east across Pendleton Moor as you steadily ascend Apronfull.

It's worth noting that the whole of Pendle and its Cloughs were used as Army, and Tank, training grounds during WW2 and afterwards

In fact the army, were still busy in the 1960's with clearing and making safe any unexploded Mines, Mortars, and shells, and even in the 70's the advice was to stick to the footpaths and not to touch or pick up anything suspicious. If you did come across something you were supposed to mark the spot and report it. However, I should confess that whilst running up Black Hill in the 80's, I kicked over half of a grenade. Ignoring advice, and judging it had already gone bang, I picked it up on my way back and dropped it off at Padiham Police Station. Much to the annoyance and grumbling of the desk sergeant who, suddenly found himself with a lot of paperwork to do.

1.5 View from Apronfull looking north west across the Ribble Valley to Longridge, Beacon, and part of the Bowland Fells.

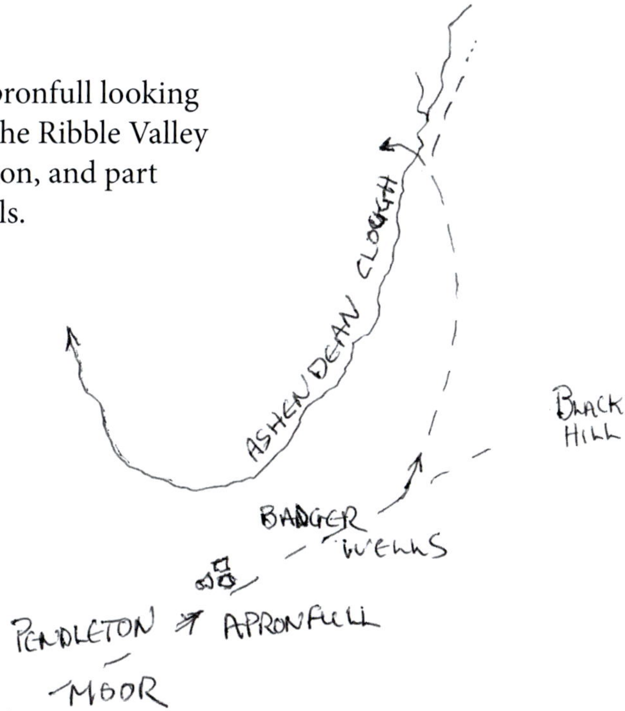

1.6 View NNW from Apronfull onto the Historic Market Town of Clitheroe and its Castle (in centre picture)

According to legend, Apronfull hill was known locally as 'Devils apronful' because it was said that the Devil became angry with the inhabitants of Clitheroe and the Castle, and in a rage he picked up an 'apronful' of large stones (from nearby Deerstones Crags) to hurl at the Castle. In doing so, he made the hole in the south east side of the Castle Keep. He emptied the remaining stones from his apron onto the ground creating a large cairn, which is barely visible today, with the stone having been taken for other use.

The hole in the Castle keep is still visible today, but in truth it was created in 1649 by agents of Cromwell's Government as part of its de-fortification plan. Skipton Castle also had its strong roofs removed so that they could no longer bear the weight of cannon

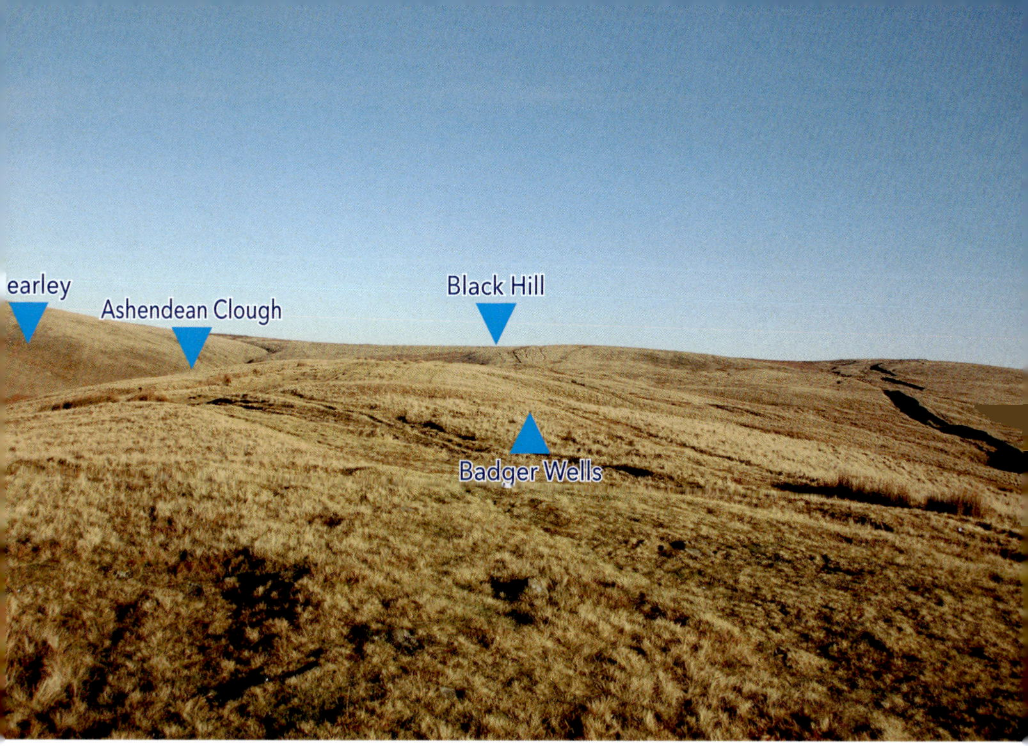

When you reach the top of Apronfull, you look directly NE across Badger Wells to the well-worn track to Black hill.

1.7 Top of Apronfull, looking across Badger Wells to Black Hill with Ashendean Clough and Mearley to the left

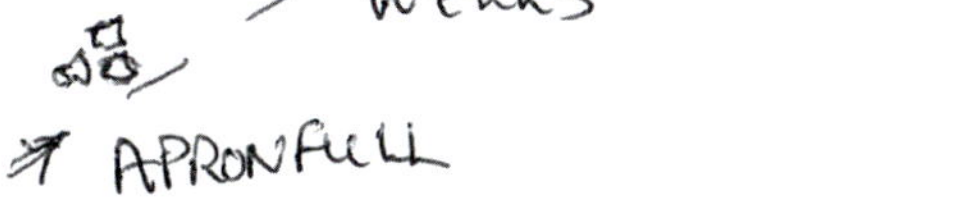

As you approach the foot of Black Hill you should take the single track to the LHS (trending N), as indicated by the way marking stone for Mearley Moor, and keeping to the RHS of Ashendean Clough.

1.8 Foot of Black Hill with LH fork up Ashendean Clough towards Mearley Moor. The 'Waymarker, or Guide stone' in the main picture is relatively new (circa 2020).

Although it's good to see the stone, it may have been nicer to have used reclaimed stone in order to give some age and character, similar to those used for the Worston moor Boundary stone and the guide stone at the Big End.

You continue to ascend until you come to a point where the track almost meets Ashendean water

1.9 Continue gradual ascent up RHS of Ashendean

Where the trod forks, bear left by a Lichen covered Boulder and crossover Ashendean Water on to Mearley Moor. Follow the track as it contours up and around to the Clayton-Le-Moors Harriers Memorial Cairn by a wall corner

1.10 Where path forks, bear left, crossover Ashendean Water on to Mearley Moor

Continue on the path come trod as it rises and contours round towards the memorial cairn

1.11 Contouring around Westwards from Ashendean towards Mearley top and the Memorial Cairn

1.11a View back to Apronfull, the Nick and Wiswell moor

Continue to the cairn

1.12 Approaching the Memorial Cairn with Longridge, Beacon, and Bowland fells in the background

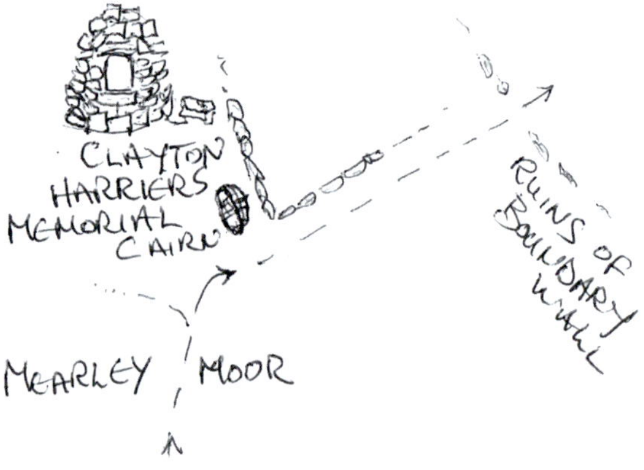

1.13 The weathered Clayton-Le-Moors Harriers memorial, to Judith Taylor and Alan Heywood. Both of whom died tragically from hypothermia whilst competing.

Judith was running the Kentmere Horseshoe Fell Race in 1994, when the situation changed to Blizzard conditions on the fell.

Alan died in the same year, on Mont Blanc. He had reached the summit, but faced horrendous weather conditions on the descent, to which he succumbed.

A reminder to us all of the dangers to which even the most experienced people can face on exposed hills, fells and mountains.

The route continues to the right of the Cairn, keeping the wall to your left crossing Mearley Moor and on to Pendle moor

1.14 View NE across Mearley moor onto Pendle moor and the Scout cairn and Shelter in the far distance

The route can be boggy in wet weather, but it dries up as you start the climb towards Scout Cairn and the shelter

Continue along the track over some boggy sections and ruined wall onto Pendle moor towards the Scout Memorial cairn and the shelter

1.15 View of Scout Memorial cairn, and Shelter from Pendle moor

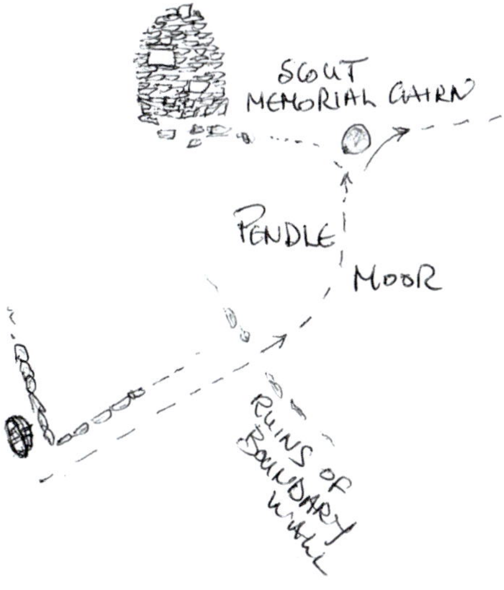

1.16 View down the Clough to Little Mearley Wood with Little Mearley Hall and farm hidden by the trees. The Hall was built late 16th Century, and it includes a two storey bay window on its frontage that is said to have come from the ruins of the nearby Sawley Abbey

1.16a Little Mearley Hall, with the two storey bay window at LHS

1.17 View from Pendle Moor of Mearley, with Clitheroe behind and Longridge Fell in the distance

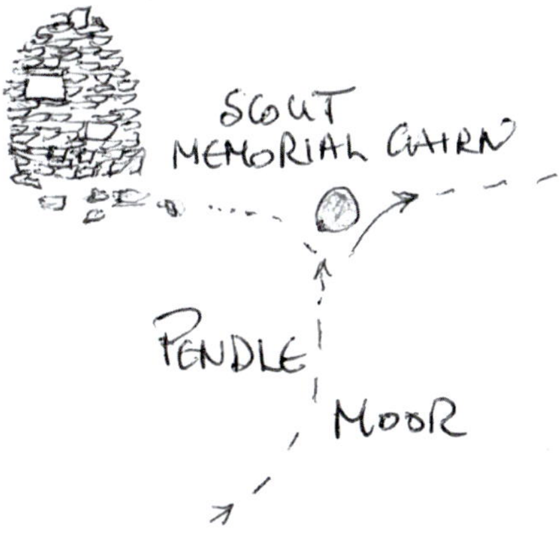

1.18 The Scout Cairn was built in 1982 to commemorate the 75th year of Scouting, with a plaque added later to commemorate the former Clitheroe Doctor and District Scout Commissioner Gordon 'Peri' Hampson who died in 1985. Additional plaques were added over the years to mark special anniversaries of the movement in the Clitheroe and District

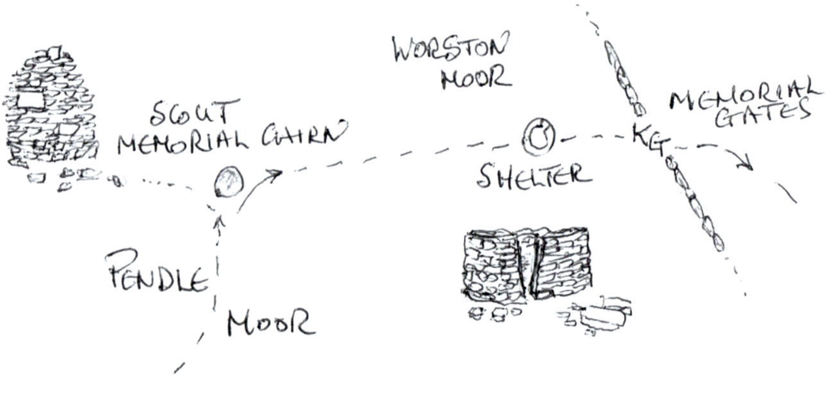

From Scout cairn follow the gently rising track trending north eastwards towards the shelter on Pendle Moor

1.19 Approaching the shelter from the SW

1.20 The substantial shelter was built in 1983.

The shelter is extremely well placed (with slotted entrance on the NE side) to protect against the prevailing SW coastal winds and gales that whip across this section of the moor

I've experienced times when you could not stand upright on this section of the moor, having to crouch almost on all fours to make progress.

My concern would be that if you were on your own taking refuge in the shelter in bad weather, you may get too comfortable and end up falling asleep.

(Looking back across Pendle moor you can see the Scout cairn as well as Mearley summit)

From the shelter continue north eastwards on the track to the memorial gate and junction of Pendle, Worston and Downham Moors

1.21 The recent Memorial gates at the junction of Pendle, Worston and Downham moors. The memorial is of a couple who first met on Pendle in the Easter of 1948

Slightly down and to the left of the gates you can see the Worston Moor Boundary stone

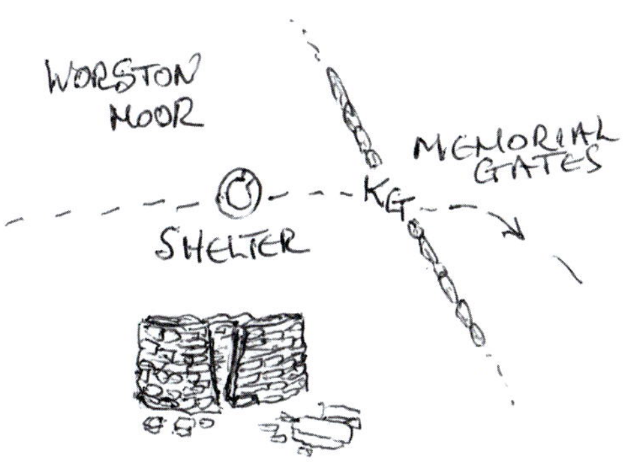

1.22 Looking NW from the memorial Gate at the top of Worston moor, on to the Hamlet of Worston, and Worsaw Hill to the right.

At 725ft, Worsaw Hill is the largest Limestone Reef Knoll in the area, with Clitheroe Castle, which also sits on one, being another.

The summit of Worsaw has what is thought to be a Bronze Age Burial Mound. A section of Roman road also ran along the East and North sides of the hill.

In the background you can see the exhaust stack of Clitheroe cement works. The cement from the works is shipped daily by road and rail. The quarry itself is well hidden and worked out parts are re wilded.

Limestone has been quarried in the area for over 400yrs, and used in building, walling and the manufacture of lime, which was produced in small lime Kilns, the remains of which can still be found dotted in and around the area today.

Crossing Pendle from East to West, the building and drystone wall material changes from Gritstone to Limestone

1.23 Looking NNW from Gate across Worston moor, to the picturesque village and estate of Downham.

Downham village is part of a private estate.

The estate changed hands a number of times, but fortunately Downham Hall has been the home of the Assheton family since the mid-16th Century, and this was a key factor in its preservation. The Hall was extended in 1835. To this day, no road markings, aerials or satellite dishes are allowed. Although the main church was built in 1910, the tower dates back to the 15th C.

Of Historical note; the forces of Oliver Cromwell were quartered in Downham in August 1648, on their way to what would be the battle of Preston. The battle was won by Cromwell's Parliamentary forces, thus ending the first Civil war.

Over the years, Downham has featured in a number of films such as – 'Whistle down the wind', 'Born and Bred', and 'Wuthering Heights'. In 2012, it also featured in the BBC Drama – 'The secret of Crickley Hall'.

1.24 View from Downham moor, over Ogden Clough, Barley moor and on to the summit trig of Pendle Hill

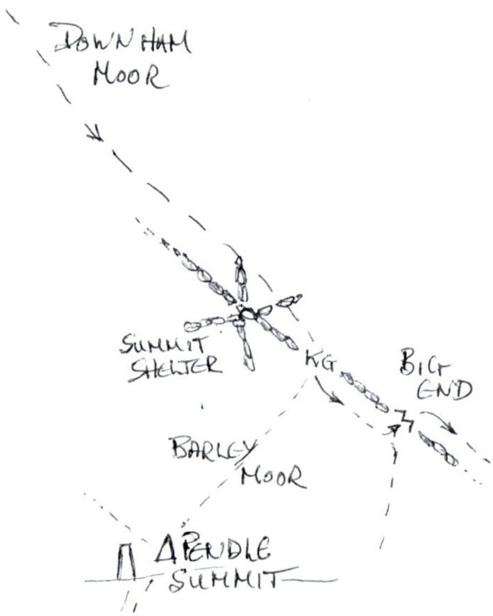

Continue along the gently rising track to the gates between Downham and Barley moors

1.25 Boundary gate from Downham moor to Barley moor with milestone on the left

1.26 Full 200x zoom long distance shot, looking approximately North West from the boundary gate and wall, over the Bowland Fells, to the South Lakeland Peaks beyond.

The route is through the kissing gate on to Barley moor and turning left, however if you look to the right you will see the Pendle summit trig and closer to, by the wall, the shelter. *For now though we leave out the summit and come back to that later on section 3*

1.27 View of Pendle Hill Summit and Trig from the boundary gate

Pendle summit is 1,827ft above sea level, so what I hear you say, it's not a Mountain, it's just a Hill! My reply would be that what it lacks in height is more than made up for in character, stature, position and reputation. It stands alone, rising steeply from its surroundings on three sides, with just the South Western side having a more gradual approach. The hill is classed as a moorland plateau and by its very nature is virtually featureless, with little to no shelter. Due to its exposed position, it is regularly lashed by high winds, driven rain and snow that, combined with wind chill can give rise to Arctic weather conditions on top. However, by contrast, on a fine clear day, you are rewarded with long reaching views out to the West coast, the Lakes and Dales to the North and the Pennine moors and Bronte country to the East.

1.28 Looking right (Westwards) from the Boundary gate you can see the Summit Shelter which was built in 2018 as part of the Pendle Hill Landscape Partnership project which is aimed at restoring and protecting the summit to minimize erosion.

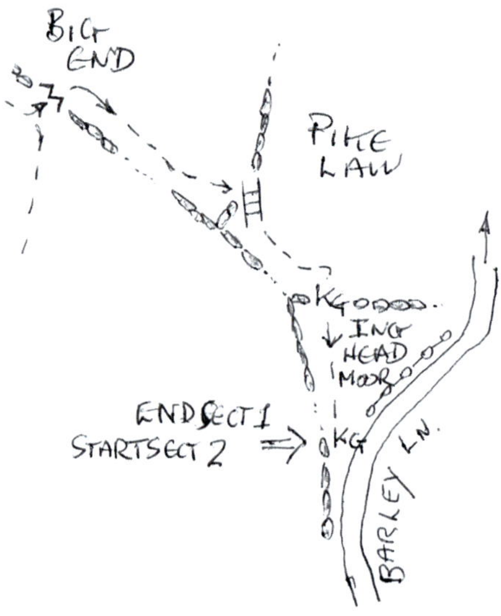

Having passed through the gate and turned left, keep the wall to your LHS as track descends about 60-70yds to the stone stile in the wall. Cross over the stile, turn immediately right, and make the steep descent (keeping the wall and fence to your right) down the big end towards Pike Law

1.29 Finger post, and Stone Stile at Big End

> If you were to cross over the stile and go diagonally right on the steeply descending trod, after about 350yds you would come to Fox's Well – see notes about that in Section 3. If you were feeling fit then its worth a detour.

1.29a Trod diagonally right to Fox's well

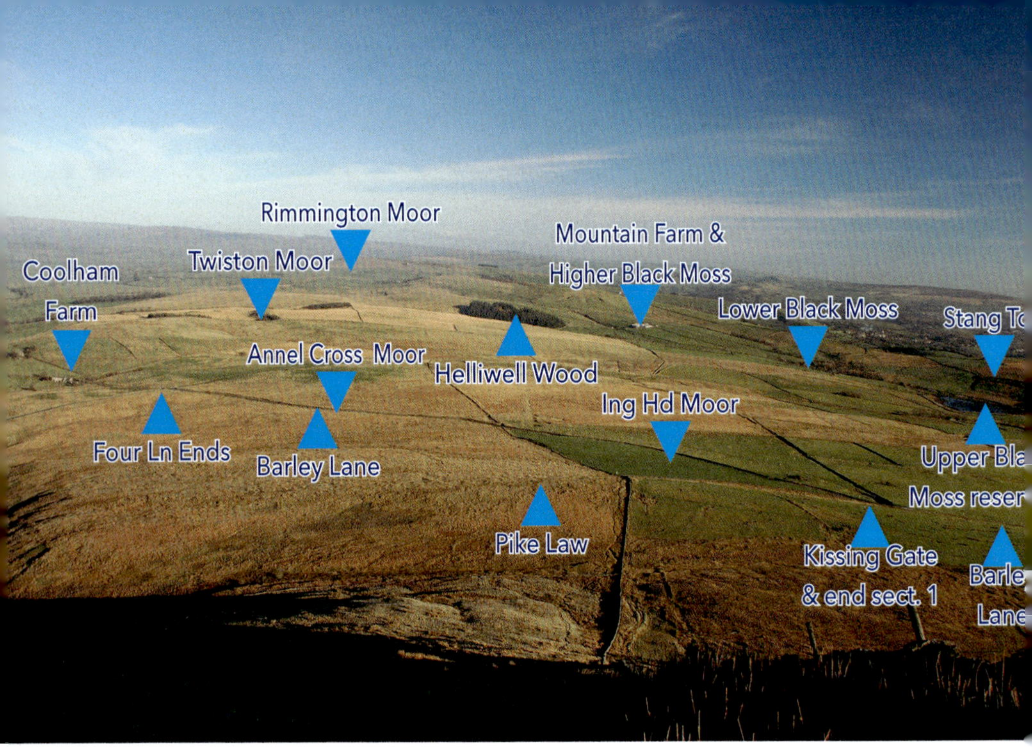

1.30 Panoramic view from Big End of descent down to Pike Law and the Kissing gate on Old Ing Moor to Barley Lane (end of Section 1).

In background you can see most of Section 2 from Four Lane Ends and Coolham Farm as far as Stang Top. Upper Black Moss reservoir is also visible middle of picture RHS.

1.30a Back of Twiston moor with a long distance shot of Coolham farm, and the Occupation lane

1.31 Ladder stile at the foot of the Big End that takes you over on to Pike Law

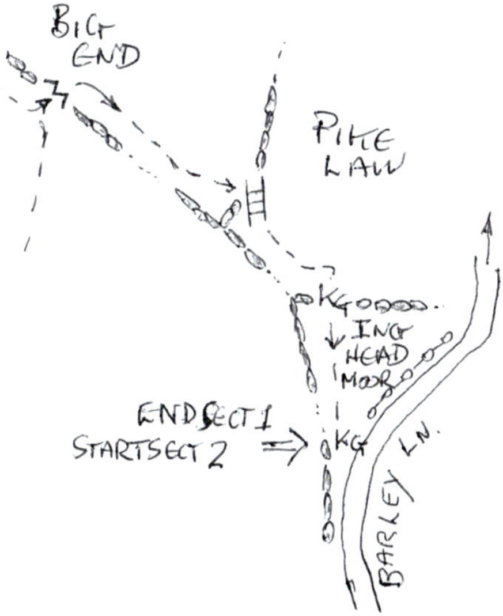

1.32 Kissing gate from Pike Law on to Ing Head Moor, with Mountain Farm on the left in the distance and Upper Black Moss Reservoir on the right

> Ing Head Moor is the smallest of all of the moors and it leads directly to the end of section 1 at the kissing gate leading to Barley lane

1.33 Kissing gate Old Ing Moor to Barley Ln and end of Section 1.

In the dip in the middle distance to the SE, you can just see the village of Barley

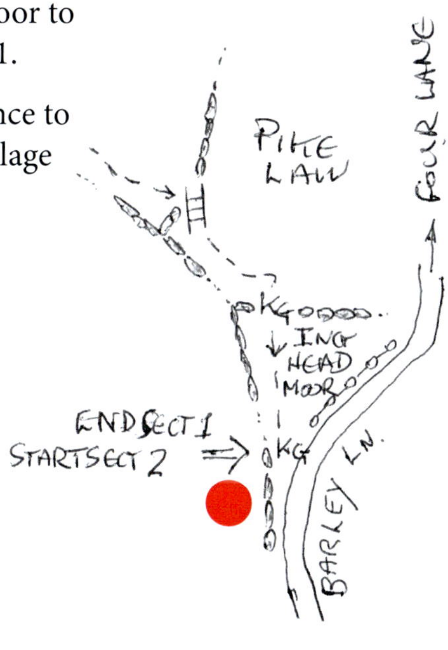

SMITHY FOLD
TWISTON
COOLHAM FARM
OCCUPATION LANE
N
DOWNHAM
ING HEAD MOOR
FOUR LANE ENDS
BLACKO
TWISTON MOOR
DUCK FLIGHT POND
KG
START SECT. 2
ANNEL CROSS MOOR
END SECT. 2
PENDLE SIDE
WINDY HARBOUR FARMHOUSE
FOOT HOUSE GATE
BARLEY
HEDGE
LOWER BLACK MOSS RESERVOIR
OVERHOUSES
BLACK MOSS WATER
PENDLE SIDE
BARLEY VILLAGE
BARLEY MOW
PLAY GROUND
CABIN, CAR PARK AND
PENDLE INN
OGDEN WATER
NOT TO SCALE

Section 2

Kissing gate Ing Head Moor (Barley Ln)

[Grid Ref.SD814 418]

on a circular route back to Pendleside (Barley Ln)

[Grid Ref.SD8145 416]

(Distance: 5.86 miles

Height gain: 946 ft)

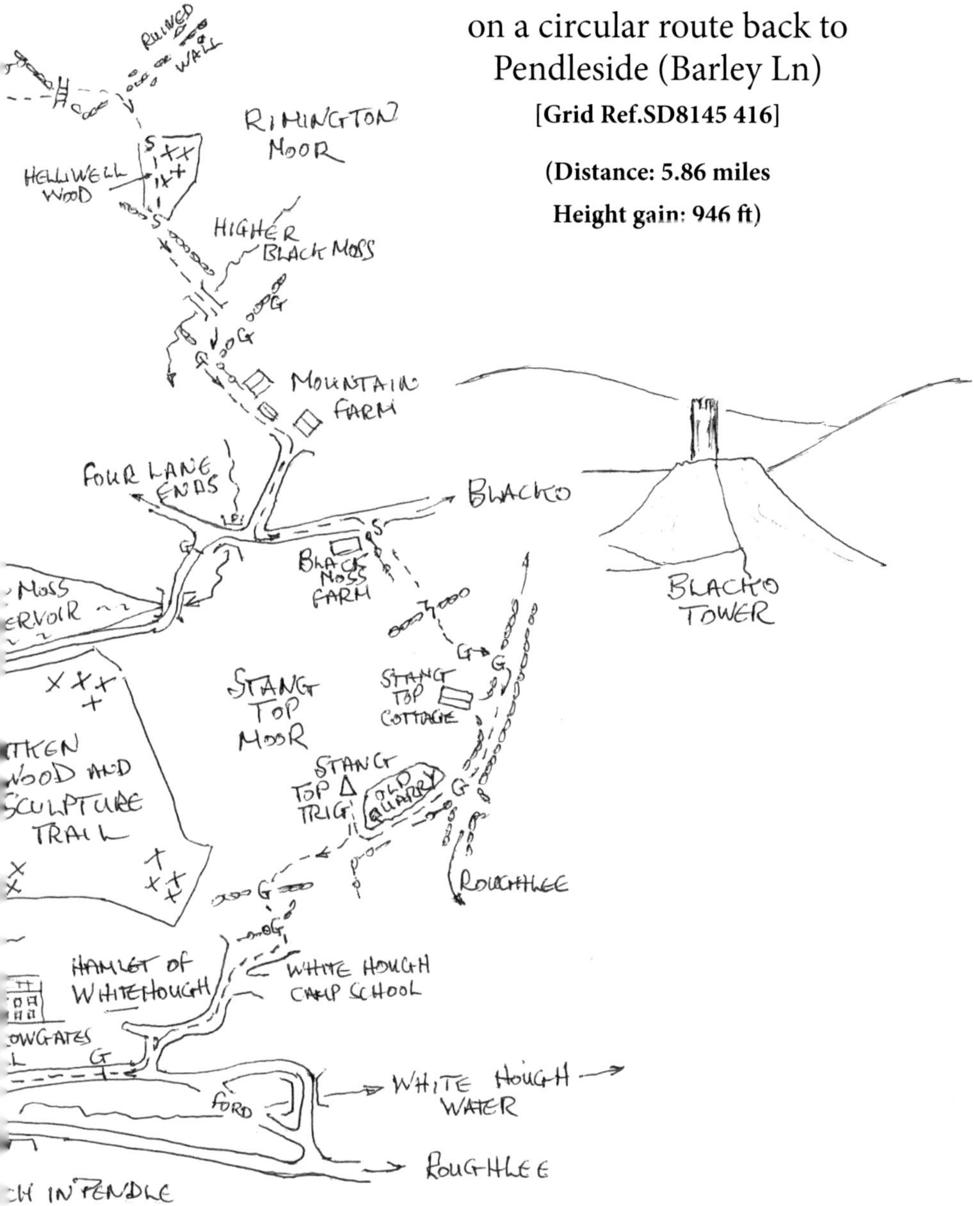

About this section

This section takes in four of the thirteen moors

There is 2/3rds mile of road at the start of this section, but the route then goes on to take in the four lower lying moors of Annel Cross, Twiston, Rimington, and Stang top as well as Helliwell wood

There is also the option to take time out at Barley Village and picnic site

The going underfoot is mixed and the paths in some areas are no more than sheep trods. The back of Twiston moor is a boggy sheep trod full of Tussock grass and reeds, as is the section from the ladder stile over to Rimington moor to Helliwell wood. In wet weather, some trods become streams. Helliwell Wood itself is wet and boggy and the path through it is indistinct, and in places crossed by fallen trees. The climb across the field up to Stang Top is usually very wet at the start.

Although, having said all of the above, *the views more than make up for it:*

Looking back from Twiston moor on a good day offers an excellent and imposing view of the northern side of the Big End as well as more far reaching views across Ribblesdale to the Longridge and Bowland fells, then onto the Yorkshire peaks of Ingleborough, Penyghent, and Fountains Fell (unfortunately, from this angle, the peak of Whernside is hidden behind Ingleborough)

The view clockwise from Stang Top takes in the classic East facing flank of Pendle, the Bowland Fells, Yorkshire Dales Peaks, Wheathead Heights, Pennine moors, Boulsworth Hill leading on to Bronte Country

Section 2 starts as you come through the kissing gate off Ing Head moor and turn left towards the four lane ends and Annel Cross Moor

2.1 Start of Section 2 looking from the kissing gate heading up the road towards the Four Lane Ends and Annel cross moor

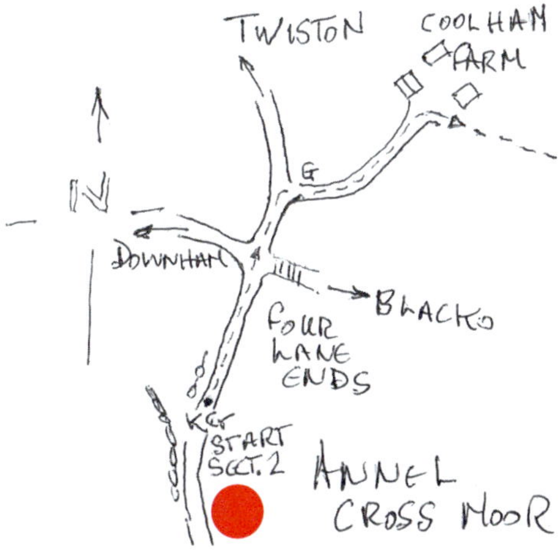

Follow the road as it tops out and then descends (with Annel Cross Moor to the right) to the Four Lane Ends where you go straight ahead signposted Twiston. The destination being Coolham Farm on the skyline in the middle distance

2.2 View as you approach the Four Lane Ends with the destination of Coolham farm in the distance

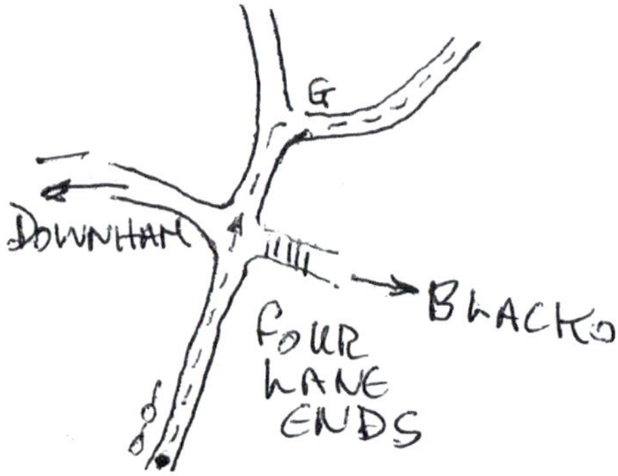

As you reach the Four Lane Ends cross roads, you can see on the left a very old milestone with finger pointers

2.3 Finger pointing milestone, or guide stone, at four lane ends. The front corner must have been broken off after its manufacture as some of the writing is also missing.

This stone should not be confused with the Annel Cross stone, which according to local maps once stood on the top of Annel Cross moor. The cross as long since gone, but if you were to pass over the cattle grid opposite and walk for 50-60yds, then cut up right onto the moor you would see the remnants, (a circular depression), of what may have been the foundations of the cross. The position of the depression does align with the position of the cross as it is shown on the 'Paths around Pendle' map.

2.4 & 2.4a When you look at the damaged milestone from the East side (see previous picture), you see a dark vertical shadow at the top of the stone. However, when you get close up and look directly down onto the top of the stone, you realise that at some time it had been drilled, as half of the hole still remains. It is likely, that this damage was done when trying to modernise the stone, which involved drilling a hole and inserting a metal pole about 3-4ft long, the top of which would have had the more modern black and white signs attached. An example of a successfully modernized stone can be seen at Dunsop Bridge, unfortunately though, the fingers on the signs are upside down.

The source of info on mile or direction stone modernization was obtained at an informal discussion with a Mr. Duncan Armstrong, who I had the pleasure to meet at his home in Padiham to discuss a possible reprint of his detailed and informative 'Paths Around Pendle, Hurst Green, Hodder bridges & Whalley Nab', map (see map full reference details on page 216). Duncan is a well known mapmaker, architect, engineer, artist and author, and he has repaired and restored many signs and finger posts in the Forest of Bowland AONB, which also includes Pendle.

Continue down the road (direction Twiston), and go through the wooden gate on the right marked Coolham. Follow the farm track round to the left and uphill to the farm (Note there was a stone stile to the left of the gate but that was found to be in disrepair and blocked off at the time of writing)

2.5 Wooden access gate and track to Coolham Farm

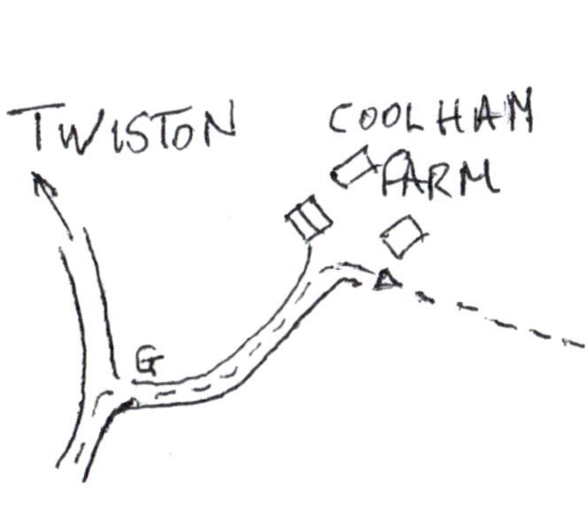

Follow the lane up towards the farm but turn right onto an ascending grass path just before the farm

2.6 Track to Coolham Farm

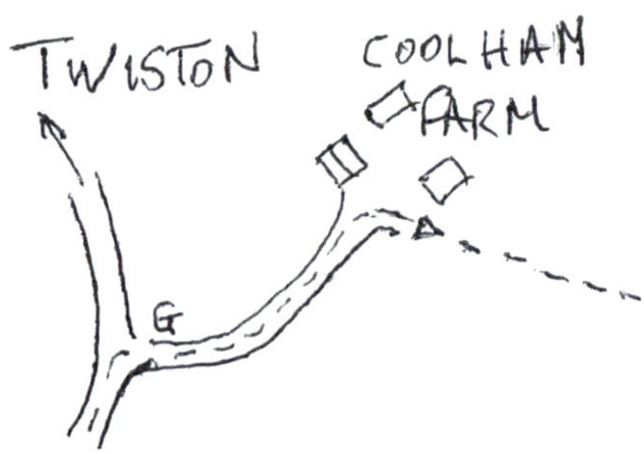

Turn right by the wall corner and fence

2.7 Approaching Coolham Farm

Please stick to the path as there is no right of way through the Farm

Turn right immediately before the farm following the green and yellow way marker on the fence by wall corner

2.8 Turning right before Coolham Farm following the directional green and yellow way marker that denotes a Public Footpath.

The track now takes us onto Twiston moor

Follow the grass trod uphill keeping the wall to the left

2.9 Continuation of path, uphill from Coolham Farm

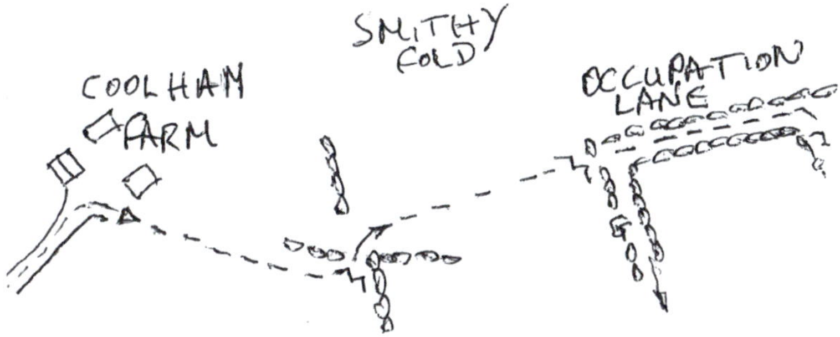

Head for the wall corner where there is a stile to the LHS of the corner

2.10 Approaching the wall corner and stile

2.10a looking back on to the Big End

Step through the stile and turn right onto a rough track

2.11 Stone stile above Coolham Farm

Follow track trending NE

2.12 track across back part of Twiston Moor

On clear days, when looking to your left, there are excellent views across Ribblesdale towards the Yorkshire Dales and Peaks. Penyghent and Ingleborough are clearly visible, but although Whernside stands the tallest of the Yorkshire 3 Peaks at 2,415ft, it is hidden from view by Ingleborough, when looking from this angle.

Continue following rough track heading towards a wall and field gate in the distance. Some way before the gate you will bear diagonally left onto a sheep trod

2.13 Continuation of track across Twiston moor

Bear left on sheep trod heading towards a tree by the wall where there is a stone stile

2.14 View along Twiston Moor, about to head diagonally left on to a sheep trod heading for the tree and the stone stile as marked by the arrow

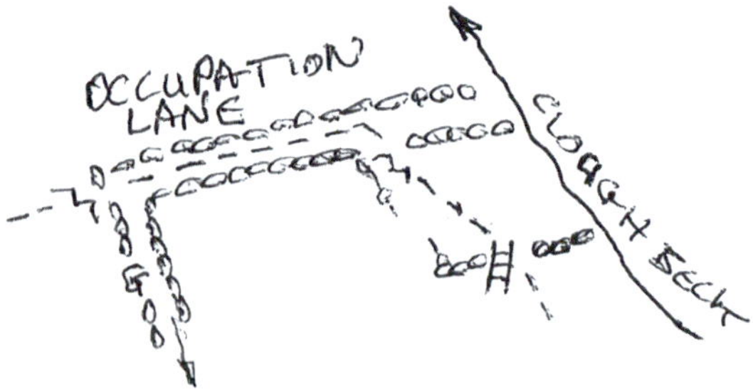

2.15 View looking NW from Twiston Moor to Higher Twiston on the left, Smithy Fold on the right and Rimington in the distance

During the 1800's there was a cotton mill at Twiston, and although most workers lived in the mill cottages, its said that a few also lived in the surrounding Hamlets, including Smithy Fold. The Mill and the cottages no longer exist, having been demolished many years ago, and the materials repurposed.

Crossover the stone stile and follow the walled ('Occupation') lane NE

2.16 Stone stile to walled occupation lane.

Occupation lanes can be found across the country as a result of the Parliamentary Inclosures Act (modern term is 'enclosure').

The act allowed for private lanes or roads (not public Highways or rights of way) to be built in order to give benefit and ease of access for occupiers of adjoining properties as well as access for mines, quarries and such like. It's not certain when and where the term 'occupation Lane' was first used but there are records of such in the 18th Century.

As well as the lanes, the act also allowed for enclosure of some previously common land. For some, this had massive social consequences, often forcing landless subsistence farmers and labourers to leave the land and find work in the mill Towns and Cities. Others argue that this is what led to the agricultural revolution that made farming more productive.

Follow the reed covered lane to its end by the trees and stile in the far distance

2.17 Looking NE along part of the Occupation lane

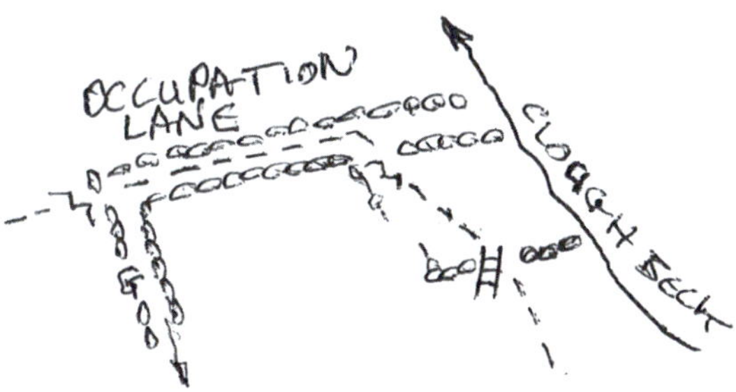

2.18a Looking North from the Occupation Lane across a cloud inversion to the Dales Peaks, from L-R Ingleborough, Penyghent and Fountains Fell

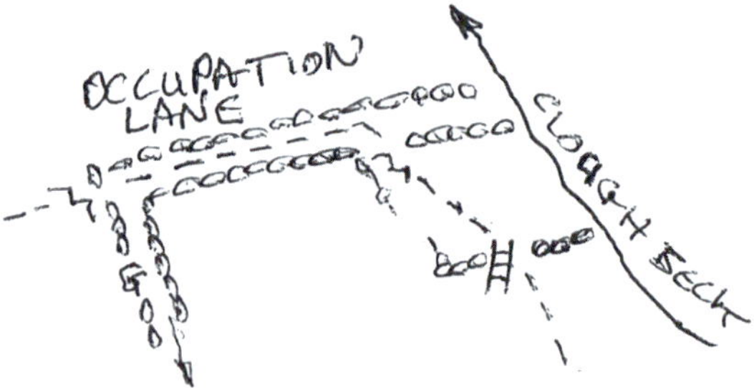

As you climb over the stone stile in the wall on the right, look up the moor, and head for a Ladder stile in the distance. There is no distinct path, just trods, tussock grass and reeds

In general, keep the fence line 3-4yds to your right

2.19 Stile at the end of the lane before the trees, to take you up the East side of Twiston Moor trending SE

Make your way up the moor with Clough Beck to the left

2.20 View up the moor to a ladder stile on the wall

As you climb over the ladder stile you can see that again there is no distinct path, just intermittent trods, small streams and reeds. However, you can't go wrong if you keep the fence to your right and head for the skyline

2.21 View over Ladder stile to the continuation up the moor

As you reach the skyline, you can see the continuation of the ascent following reed covered trods through newly planted trees. Keep the fence about 3-5yds to your right

2.22 Continuation up the moor following trods through newly planted trees

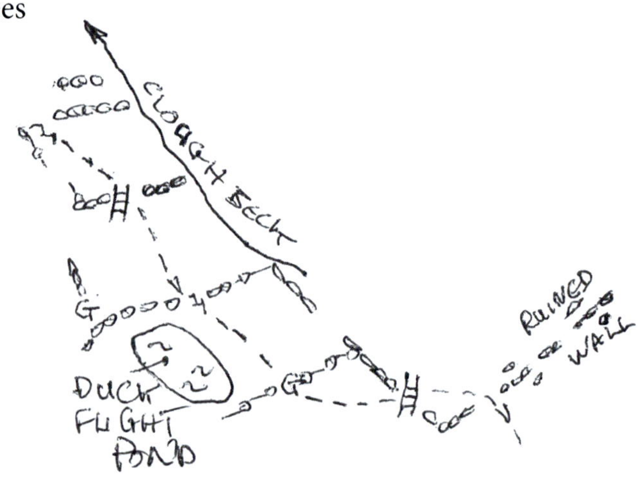

As you leave the trees behind, you head, still following trods, towards a fence and wall line

There is a stone stile, that's not easily spotted, by a fence post

2.23 Continuation up the moor following trods to stone stile in the wall ahead

The barely visible stone stile, is next to the fence post, which is used as a support to help you over the stile

2.24 Stone stile – not easily spotted

Climb over the stile keeping the pond to your right. As you skirt the pond, head towards the skyline keeping parallel with the wall on your left, and you will come to a wooden gate.

2.25 View up the moor following intermittent trods, with a wildlife and duck flighting pond on the right. The destination is shown by the arrow just off centre on the skyline

Go through the gate and follow the trod through the reeds, heading for the centre skyline where the trees look to meet the wall on the left

2.26 Continuation through the gate and up the moor following the trod through the reeds

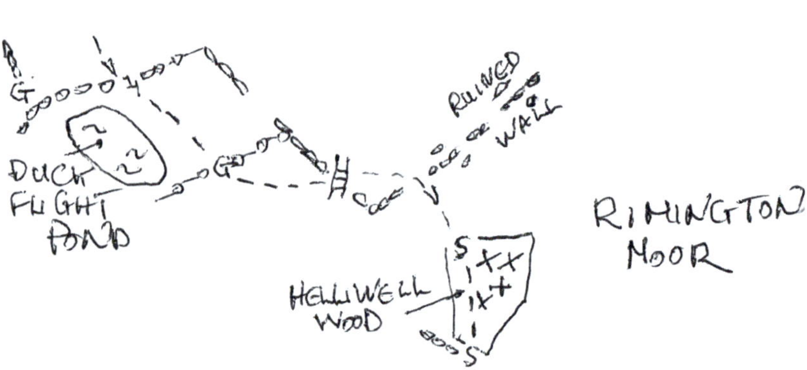

Continue following the trod heading towards the trees and wall, and eventually reaching the top where there is a ladder stile to take you over on to Rimington moor

2.27 Top of the climb of this side of the moor with ladder stile for crossing over on to Rimington moor

On a good day, looking northwards across Ribblesdale from the stile, you can see some of the Yorkshire Dales peaks.

On this particular day, Ribblesdale was covered by a cloud inversion with only the tops of the peaks visible.

(from L-R Ingleborough, Penyghent and Foutains Fell)

Whilst out running one day with my Daughter in Law Katie, I stopped to take in this particular view, and happened to comment that it would make a great photo in guide book of the area, to which Katie replied "why don't you get on and write one then".

2.28 Long distance shot over the top of a cloud inverted Ribblesdale to some of the Yorkshire peaks, From L-R Gragareth, Ingleborough, Penyghent, and Fountains Fell. Whernside is hidden from this angle by Ingleborough

The route continues over the stile turning right, trending SE, and heading down towards the RH corner of Helliwell wood. Keep the wall and fence about 15-20yds to your right following boggy, reed covered trods

2.29 Rimmington side of stile looking towards Helliwell Wood

It is quite common to see wild deer roaming in and around this part of the moors

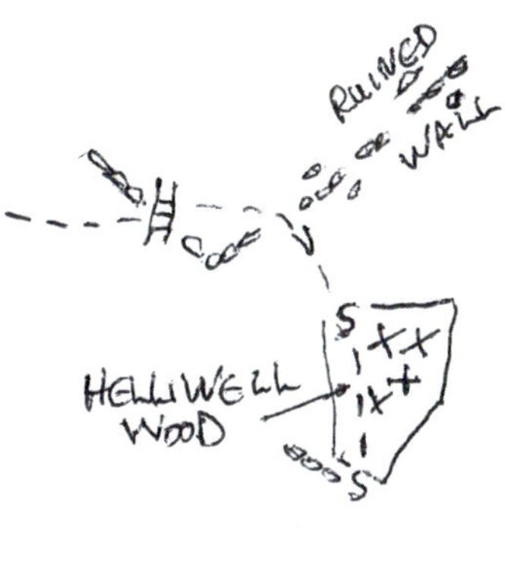

Approaching Helliwell wood with stile in Bottom right corner

2.30 Continue following trod to stile at the right hand corner of the wood

I have tried to establish how Helliwell and Aitken Woods (planted circa mid 1930's) got their names.

The surname Helliwell is of Yorkshire origin, and popular in the nearby town of Todmorden, but I could not find anyone of note locally with that name. United Utilities were helpful, but they were also unable to shed any light on the naming of the wood.

The surname Aitken is, in the main, Scottish in origin, and it's common in the Lowland and border regions. However, there was an Aitken family in the area who were land owners in the Black Moss area, and so it's possible the wood was named after them.

Pass over the stile into the wood. The trods are intermittent but you are still trending SE, heading towards daylight and a gate and stile on the other side.

2.31 Stile leading in to Helliwell Wood

Still heading for the daylight

2.32 View looking South East through the start of the wood to the daylight at the other side

The route opens up and the path becomes clearer

2.33 The path becomes clearer as you get towards the far side of the wood

> As you pass through the wood, depending which trod you take, you may see evidence of various camp craft activities such as shelter building, fire pits and benches.
>
> It could be the work of students from the Whitehough Camp School.

Almost out of the wood.

2.34 Approach to the exit of the wood

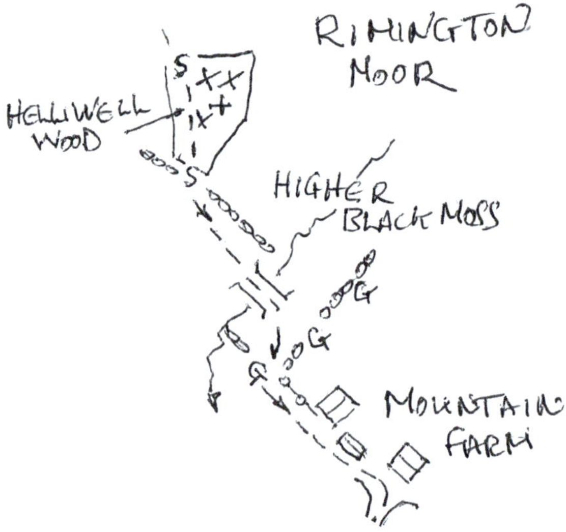

As you exit the wood, the gate and stile come into view. Pass over the stile and turn immediately left following the wall and track to Higher Black Moss

2.35 Stile to Higher Black Moss, with view across to Aitken wood on the left in the distance

Direction Higher Black Moss

2.36 Track to Higher Black Moss with Mountain Farm in the distance

As you dip down into Higher Black Moss, cross the bridge, and take a right, as signposted, for Lower Black Moss, then turn left and walk uphill alongside the right of the agricultural buildings of Mountain Farm

2.37 Approach to Higher Black Moss

2.38 Sign for Lower Black Moss. This is what you would call a 'proper' sign, and is in memory of – Roy 'stretch your legs' Clarke.

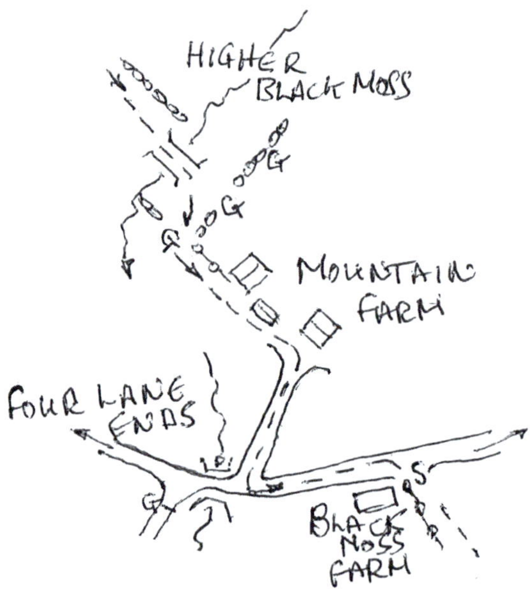

As you bear right on the track after 20-30yds pass through a gate turning left onto an uphill track, with fence to your left, and heading towards the agricultural buildings on the RHS. Continue along the right side of the buildings towards the farm

2.39 Uphill track towards Mountain Farm

2.40 Route goes along RHS of buildings

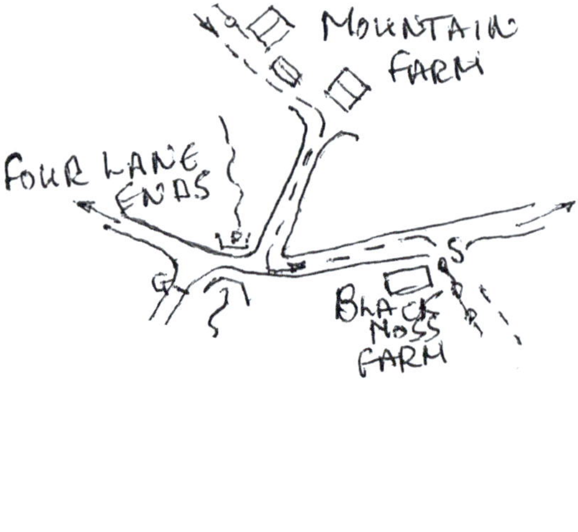

2.41 Continuation of track towards Mountain Farm

As you come to the end of the buildings cross the front of the farmyard, turning right onto the farm track that descends down to Lower Black Moss

2.42 Looking down the track from Mountain Farm to Lower Black Moss and road. In the distance L-R are Stang Top, Aitken Wood and Upper Black Moss reservoir

Stang Top moor and cottage can be seen on the skyline at the LHS of the picture

2.43 Lower Black Moss where the Mountain Farm Track meets Black Moss Rd

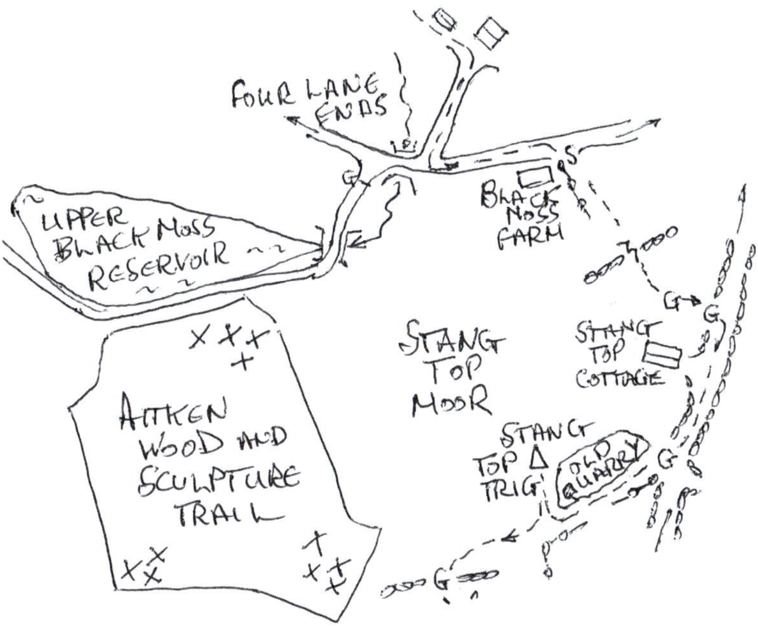

As you meet Black Moss road turn left and follow the road uphill for about 150yds, past Black Moss Farm to a stile on your right

2.44 Black Moss road

Cross the stile and head diagonally up across the field to Stang Top Cottage on the skyline. The first section of the field is wet, but the higher up you get, the drier it becomes

2.45 Stile on Black Moss Road looking to the South East towards Stang Top Cottage on the skyline

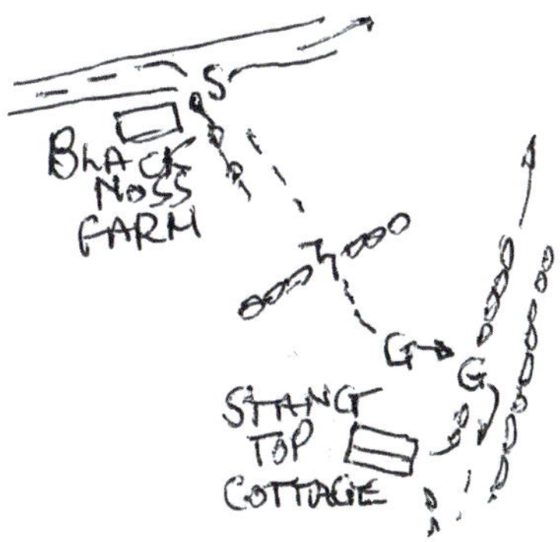

2.46 Arrow showing the position of stile on skyline

Once over the stile, the going can initially, be wet and boggy, but it soon becomes firm.

There is no clear path or trod until you get close to the stile, so just aim for the arrow on the skyline

As you approach the stile the path becomes clear. Crossover the stile and head diagonally left

2.47 Wall stile to Stang Top Cottage

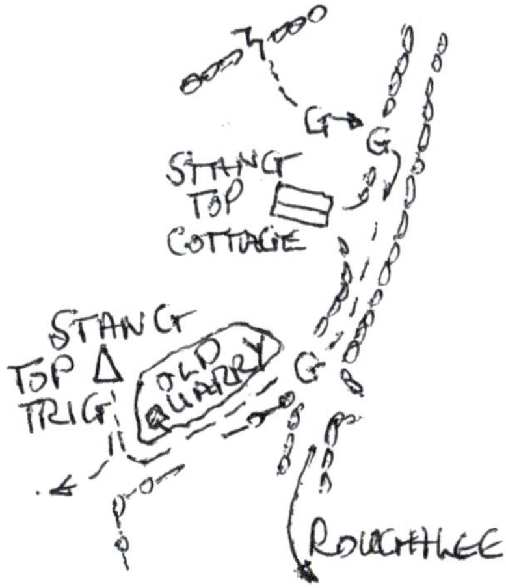

Head towards the tree on the skyline, and then go through the pedestrian gate to the right of the tree

2.48 View towards Stang Top Cottage

2.49 Gate into garden of Stang Top Cottage

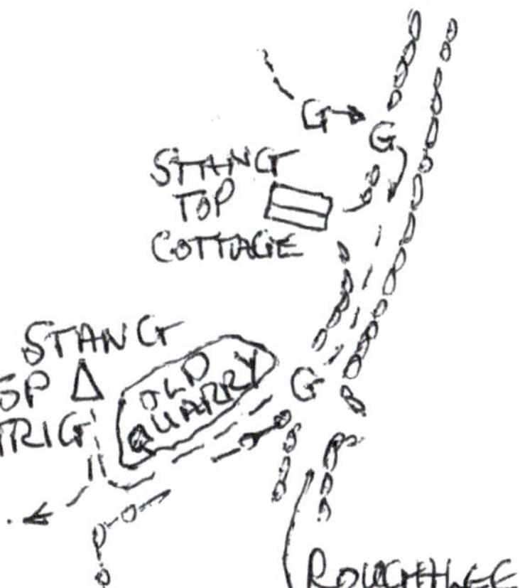

Please cross the garden diagonally right in single file, respectfully and in good time, as whilst it is a right of way it is also someone's garden. The way forwards onto Stang Top road is by one of the smallest gates I've ever seen. Once through the gate turn right and follow Stang Top road uphill. ***Beware of oncoming traffic as you approach the crest of the road.***

2.50 Small gate at the exit from the garden

2.51 View looking back across the garden on to the Eastern flank of Pendle Hill

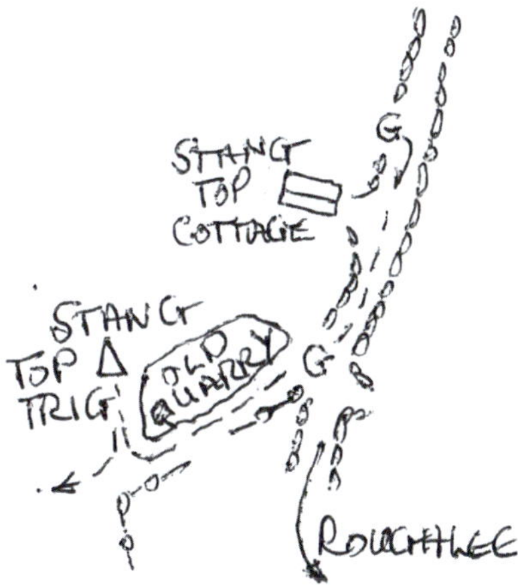

2.52 View from Stang Top Cottage Garden looking East onto Blacko Hill and Tower. The village of Blacko is in the centre right of the picture.

Blacko Tower, or Stansfield Tower as it is also known, is a 'Folly' and was built in 1890 by local businessmen Jonathan Stansfield. It's a circular castellated tower, built in rough stone, and standing about 30ft high.

The history behind the tower is not clear, but the most common understanding was that Mr. Stansfield wanted to be able to look across into Ribblesdale and hence commissioned the tower to be built. However, on completion, Mr. Stansfield was disappointed as the finished tower was nowhere near tall enough. It's unclear whether the calculation of the height that the Tower needed to be was wrong, or whether it was supposed to be higher, and he just ran out of money?

Continue uphill taking care for oncoming traffic

2.53 Continuation of route up Stang Top Road

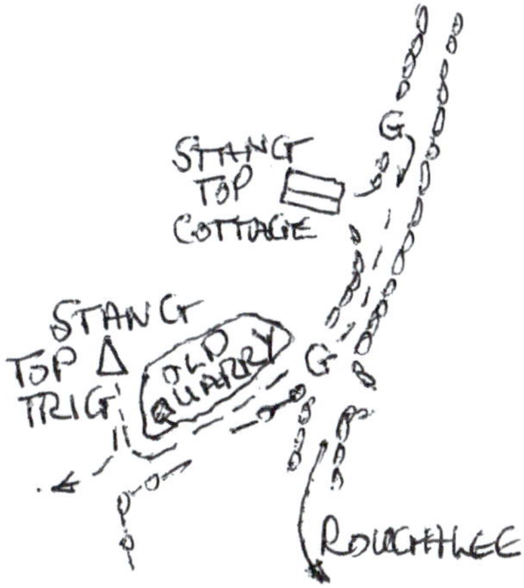

2.54 Looking back from the crest of Stang Top road to Helliwell Wood, Higher Black Moss and Mountain Farm

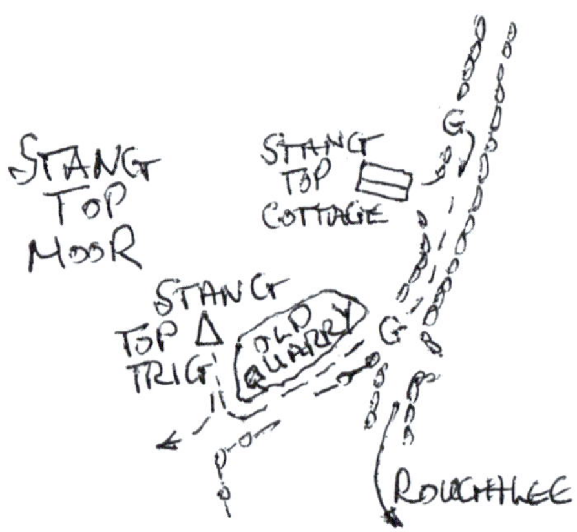

As you top out on the crest of the road, you should pass through the metal field gate on the right, and follow the sign post along a muddy track

2.55 Crest of Stang Top road with gate to Stang Top and Trig

Within a 50-60yards you come to a disused and overgrown quarry to the right, with Stang Top Trig visible. Continue along the muddy track to the end of the quarry and then cut off uphill to the right to the trig before doubling back to rejoin the muddy track

2.56 Stang Top quarry with Trig point visible on the crest (in centre of picture)

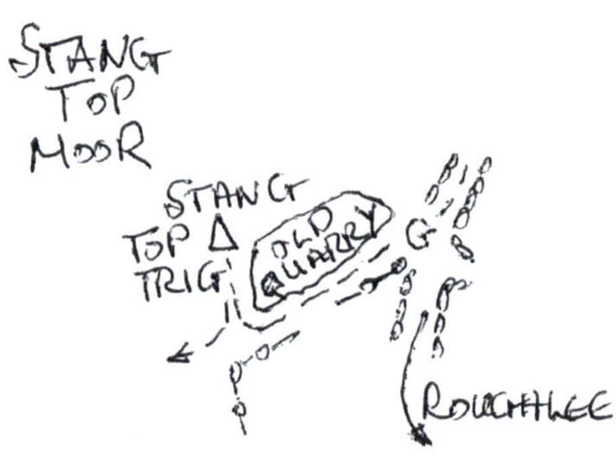

2.57 View of East flank of Pendle from Stang Top Trig at 1,076ft (328m)

In 2015, someone saw fit to paint it in Claret and Blue, the colours of the local football club – Burnley FC.

Maybe it was in recognition of the fact that Burnley FC were promoted back (after a four year absence) to the Premier League for the 2014–2015 season? However, the season did not end well, with Burnley FC being relegated.

Once back on the muddy track follow it downhill keeping the fence on your left

2.58 Continuation of muddy track

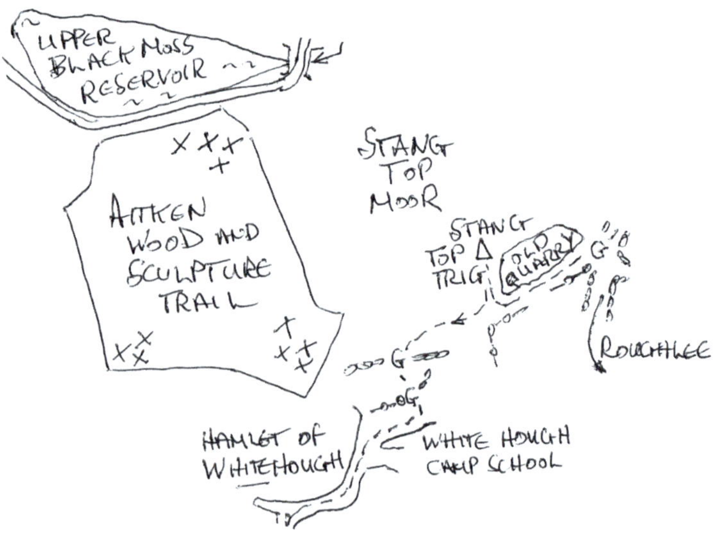

When the fence and track end, follow the path to a muddy trod downhill making for a gate close to the left hand edge of the conifer wood and in the direction of Whitehough.

2.59 View of muddy trod down to Whitehough

Continue along and when the path come trod forks, take the left grassy path downhill

2.60 Continuation of path down towards Whitehough

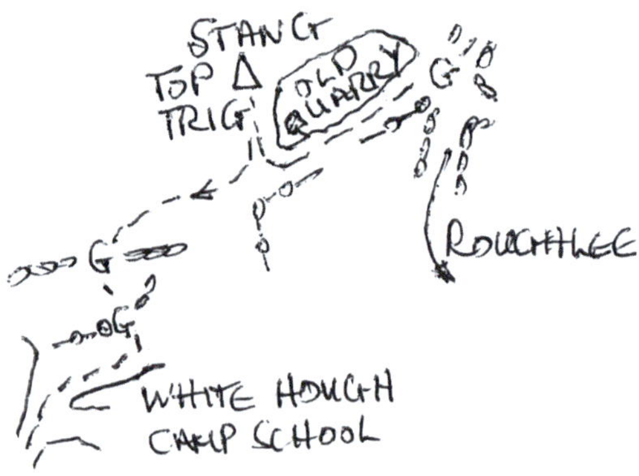

Take the left, grassy trod downhill towards the gate trending for the point marked by the arrow

2.61 Continued path down to Whitehough.

Head for gate in wall (to right of centre picture)

2.62 View looking down to towards Whitehough

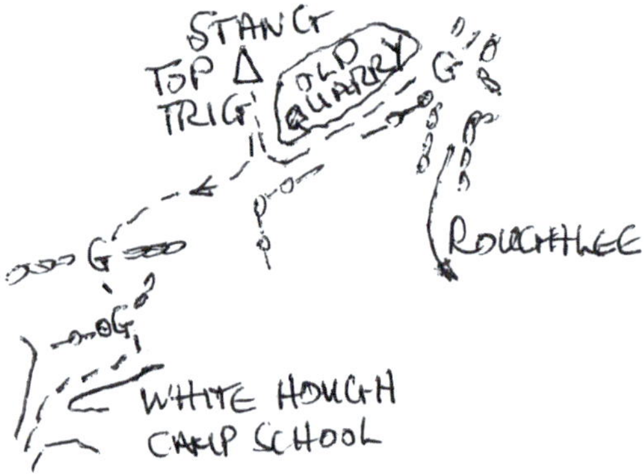

Go through gate, passing through a small plantation to a wooden gate leading to Whitehough Outdoor Centre.

2.63 Gate towards Whitehough

Pass through a wooden gate and turn right heading for Whitehough. You're going to be following the road downhill and through the hamlet to a T-junction by White Hough water.

2.64 Wooden gate leading to Whitehough Outdoor Centre and the Hamlet of Whitehough.

Continue past the back of some of the Whitehough Outdoor Centre buildings turning left onto road, and passing the two entrances to the Centre

2.65 Approach alongside the outbuildings at the back of Whitehough Outdoor Centre

2.65a Camp School

2.66 Whitehough 'Camp School' as it used to be called was opened by Nelson Council in 1938 and it was intended that every Nelson child would, at some point in their school life, spend 1–2 weeks there in clean air.

In 2015, Lancashire County Council, the then owners, closed it. However, it was fortunate that in 2017, 'Burnley FC in the Community' (BFCitC) acquired the lease and reopened it as the Outdoor Centre, which they now run.

The first Head of the 'camp school' was Kenneth Oldham, who took up post in 1956 and stayed until his retirement in 1983. Kenneth saw 50,000 children attend his courses, and he led expeditions to amongst other places, the Alps, Dolomites and Iceland. In 1951, whilst at his previous school on the edge of the Peak District, Kenneth led the first school party to walk the 270 mile Pennine Way, and in 1960 he wrote the first guidebook for the Way, a full 5yrs before it was designated Britain's first long distance footpath. Kenneth was awarded an MBE for his life's work.

Continue down the road, through the hamlet of Whitehough, and eventually bearing left towards the T junction

2.67 Road down to Hamlet of Whitehough

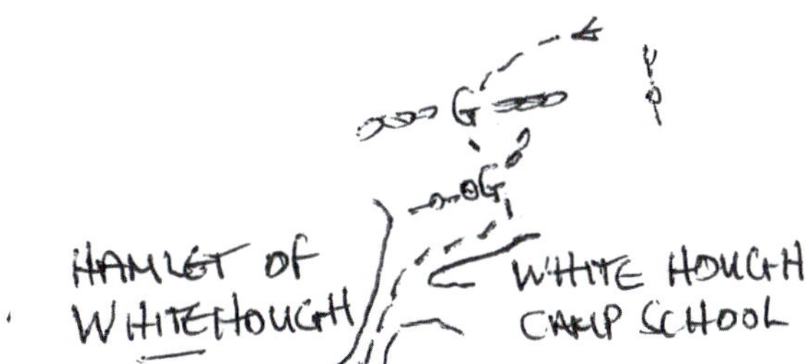

Having passed through Whitehough Hamlet you will approach the T junction by the side of White Hough Water where you will turn right.

2.68 Approaching the T junction where you turn right for Barley Village via the Hamlet of Narrowgates

Of interest, White Hough Water comes into being where Barley water joins Pendle water in front of Barley Village Hall, and at its other end, in the village of Roughlee, it becomes Pendle water again.

Pendle Water, goes on to pick up Blacko water on its way to the villages of Higherford and Barrowford, where it picks up Colne and Walverden Waters before its confluence with the River Calder near Burnley.

In August 1967 there was terrible flooding which damaged bridges in Barley and wreaked havoc in the downstream villages of Higherford and Barrowford. Flooding was also recorded in 1992 and 2,000.

Turn right at the junction and follow the gated track, with White Hough Water to your left

2.69 Gated track leading to Barley village via the Hamlet of Narrowgates

2.70 Continuation along track, through the gates

2.71 Track approaching the Hamlet of Narrowgates with Narrowgates House set back on the right

Bollard Wood on your right, was more than likely named after the Bollard family who were landowners in Whitehough and the Barley with Wheatley Booth areas.

Continue along the road past the Cottages and the Mill

2.72 The Hamlet of Narrowgates with its terraced Mill Cottages and Mill.

The Cotton Mill was built in 1799 and powered at the time with a modern water turbine.

The Mill changed ownership many times over the years, and eventually closed in 1967, having been run by the Metcalfe family for more than 50yrs.

The Mill was converted into residential accommodation and the cottages were renovated and modernised in 1976 by Pendle Council. There was another mill at Barley Green, but that was badly damaged by severe floods in 1880 and never reopened. Nelson Corporation bought the site and in 1912 opened the Nelson water treatment works which operated until its closure in 2007 when it was converted in to the private dwellings that you see today.

As you leave Narrow Gates, take a path to the right of the track which leads directly to Barley Village carpark and picnic site

2.73 Track to Barley Village, carpark and picnic site

The old mill pond for Narrowgates mill was filled in many years ago to form part of the car park you see today

The picnic site is more than half way round the walk and as such is a good resting/refreshment point

2.74 Barley car park, Toilets, Cabin Café, and Picnic site

The car parking facility is large compared to the size of the village, but that is a sign of the popularity of the area and Pendle Hill. At weekends, holidays and some events, it is common to find the car park full, along with the roadside parking as far as the eye can see. To be relatively sure of a place at busy times you need to be there by latest 08.00hrs.

Close by is Boothman Park which is said to offer fishing, archery, walking, bird watching, deer watching and amazing photographic opportunities.

The route continues past the picnic site, over the bridge and heading in a NNW direction through the village

2.75 View from the, Cabin Café area to picnic site and village

In the village there is the Pendle Inn and Barley Mow, with both offering good food, drinks and accommodation.

Some of the services in the car park/picnic area, or close by

2.76a

2.76b

2.76c

2.76d Path from Picnic site to the village via a bridge over Barley water

2.79

2.80

The route continues through the village trending NNW

2.81 View through village looking NNW and in the distance is the turning on the right for Black Moss

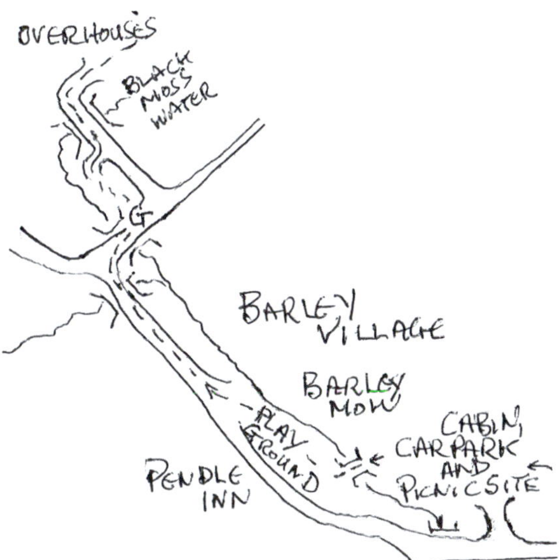

At the end of the village turn right on to the track for Black Moss reservoirs following the sign for Blacko

2.82 Turning for Black Moss reservoirs, sign posted Blacko

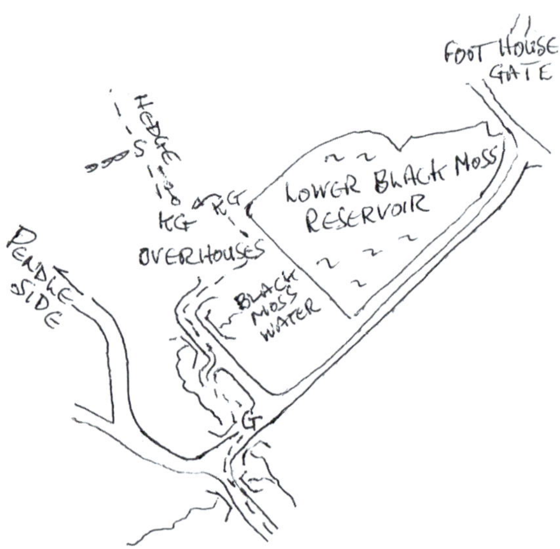

As you cross the bridge, follow sign posted path on the left, through kissing gate, for the Hamlet of Overhouses

2.83 View uphill along Black Moss reservoir access road

> Note: if you were to follow the road up the hill you would pass Lower Black Moss reservoir, the Dam of the upper reservoir, and then on the right would be Aitken Wood and the entrance to the Sculpture Trail

As you cross the bridge turn left through the kissing gate and follow the path alongside Black Moss water

2.84 Through the kissing Gate to the start of the path to Overhouses

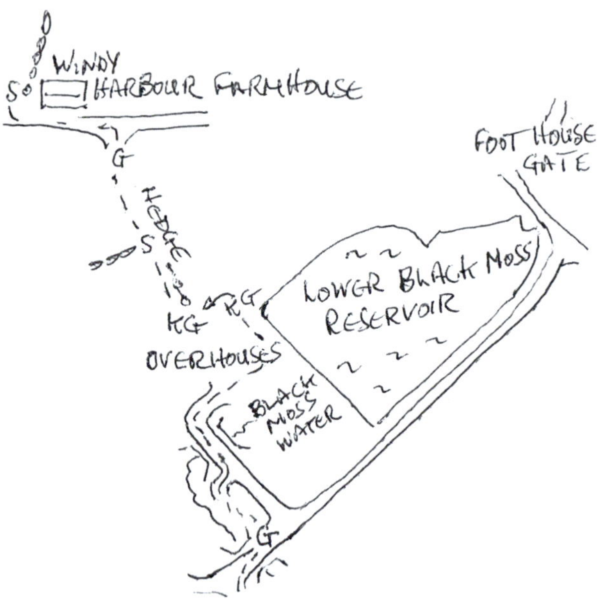

As you approach the bridge and road to Overhouses go through gate and turn left over the bridge

2.85 Gate leading to Overhouses

Cross the bridge and bear right into Overhouses

2.86 Road bearing right to Overhouses

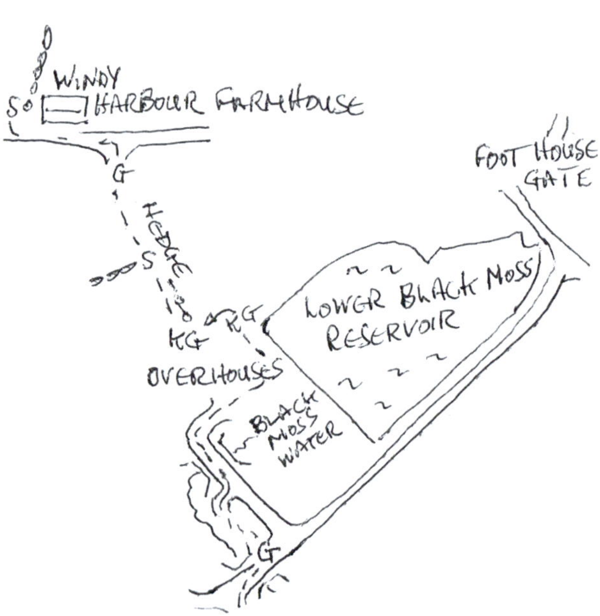

Continue straight ahead onto a grass track by Overhouses Lower Barn house

2.87 View of route straight ahead past Overhouses lower Barn House, with lower Black Moss Reservoir Dam behind. The 17th century cottage is buried to the left of the tree

Follow the track through field keeping the fence and then the wall to the right and continue upwards to a kissing gate

2.88 Track bearing round to left heading towards Windy Harbour. Black Moss Lower Reservoir Dam can be seen in the background.

In 2011, workers for United Utilities uncovered the remains of a buried Cottage under a mound below the Dam. The 'discovery', just before the 400th Anniversary of the 1612 Lancashire Witch Trials, caused quite a stir. With some saying that it was the long lost Malkin Tower – the meeting place of the Witches Coven. The remains were excavated and examined by historians and archaeologists, who confirmed it was of 17th Century origin. However, it seems the cottage had never been lost, just partly demolished and smoothed over in 1902 to make way for the reservoir. Historians are divided on whether or not it was 'Malkin Tower', so for now it just adds to the local folklore. The cottage was documented and recorded in detail, and then carefully recovered to prevent further looting.

Go through kissing gate and turn immediately left

2.89 View of kissing gate where you turn left for Windy harbour

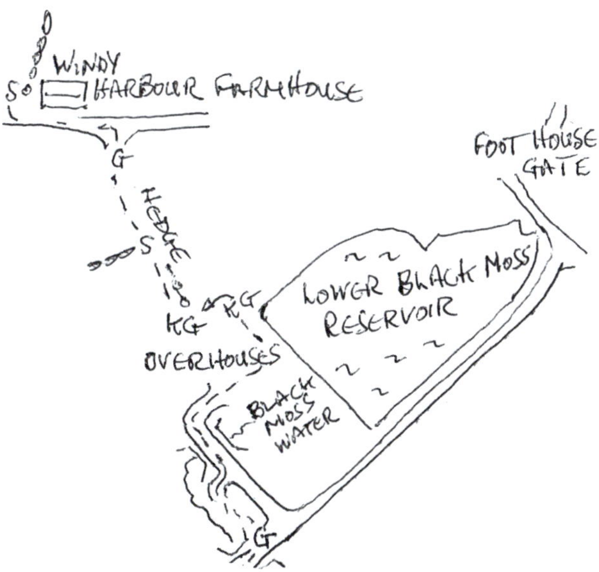

In a few yards you come to another Kissing gate where you turn right and uphill to Windy harbour

2.90 Go through the kissing gate and turn immediately right, continuing uphill to Windy Harbour

Follow trod uphill towards Windy Harbour keeping fence, Hedge and stream to right

2.91 Uphill trod and path to Windy Harbour

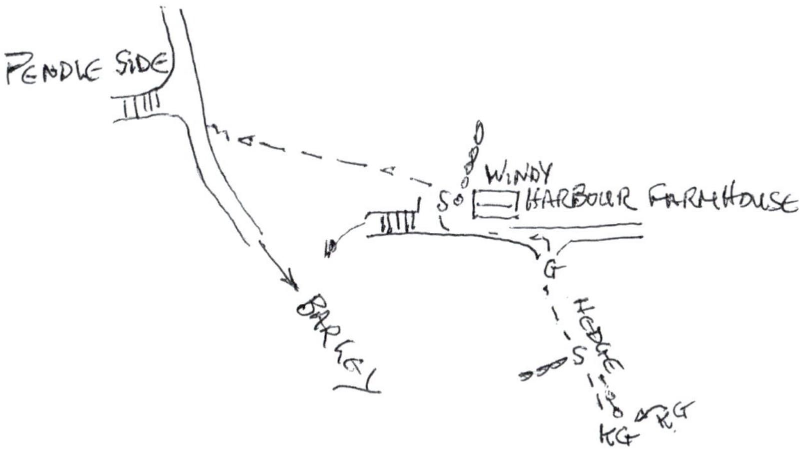

Pass over stile and continue uphill to gate to Windy Harbour

2.92 Stile on the way up to Windy Harbour

On two occasions after crossing over the stile I have put up a Hare, which must have been taking cover in the hedge to the right.

The way forwards is to go through the kissing gate and turn left, passing Windy Harbour House on the right

2.93 Approach to kissing gate leading to Windy Harbour House

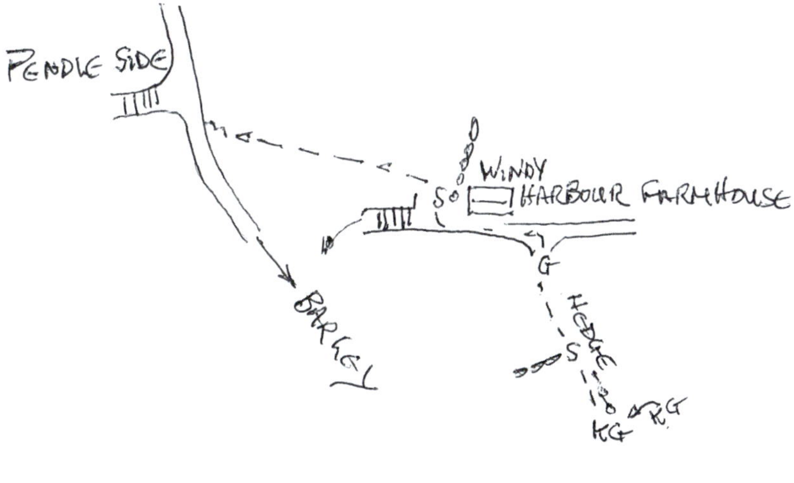

Walk Past the house on the slightly descending track towards a cattle grid

2.94 View past Windy Harbour House towards cattle grid

The name 'Windy Harbour' or 'Windy Arbour', is unusual for the area, but it could be that it's named after the small village of the same name in Ireland. Alternatively, 'Arbour' was associated with Roman roads as being places to take shelter along the way, however, with the nearest Roman road being 2-3 miles away, that looks to be unlikely.

In addition, just down the track from Windy Harbour is 'Salt Pie' Farm, which is another unusual name. The type of houses with 'lean to' buildings on the side, have, in years by, been referred to as Salt Pie as they resemble the wooden, sloping top, salt storage boxes that used to be fastened on the wall in a kitchen. Another possibility is that the farm took deliveries of salt piles from the Cheshire mines and then distributed it to other farms for use in meat preservation.

Well before the cattle grid, turn right onto small grassed area with step over stile on the back right hand side by the wall

2.95 Small grassed area with step over stile leading to field

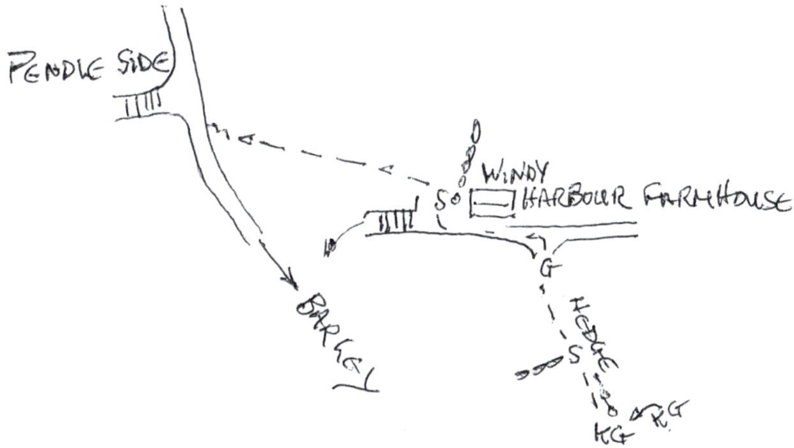

Cross over the stile turning diagonally left in the direction of Barley lane and Pendleside

2.96 Wooden stile to Pendleside

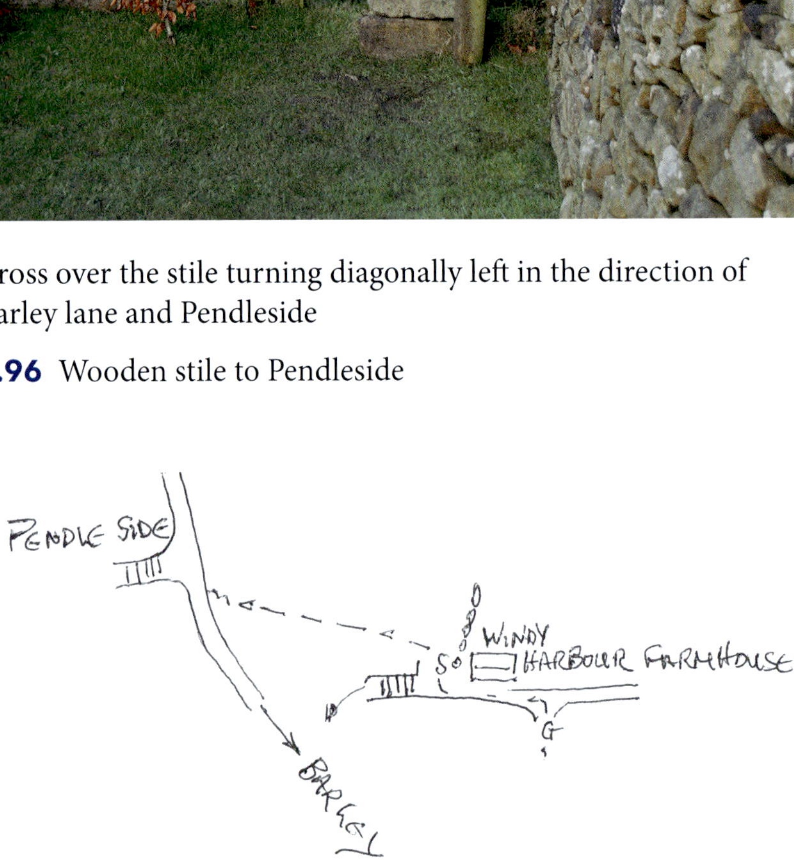

Once over the stile head diagonally left, heading for a stone stile to Barley Lane and Pendleside, marked on the skyline with an arrow

2.97 View over stile to Pendleside and Barley lane on the skyline (Note the unusual cloud shrouding the profile of Pendle and the Big End)

These cloud formations are known as 'Orographic Clouds', which need a certain set of conditions to form, starting with a cool wind being driven over a plain or plateau. As the cool, wind driven air meets a hill or mountain its starts to rise and chill as it goes.

When conditions are right, the lower air close to the ground can create water droplets which in turn form a layer of cloud that appears to hug the landscape. On the Leeward side, the cloud can often be seen to run off the landscape like waterfall. The formation is regularly seen on Table Top mountain in South Africa, and they call the phenomenon the 'Table Cloth'.

Cross over the stile onto Barley Lane and turn right. Walk a few yards uphill to Pendleside on the left

2.98 Stone stile to Barley Lane and Pendleside

Pendleside and the end of Section 2/start of Section 3

2.99 Turning for track to Pendleside

Section 3

Pendleside (Barley Ln)

[Grid Ref.SD8145 416]

to Nick o' Pendle, crosso
ver to Wiswell Moor Tri
and back to the Nick o'
Pendle (Clitheroe Rd)

[Grid Ref.SD7725 386]

(Distance: 6.83 miles

Height gain: 1,444 ft)

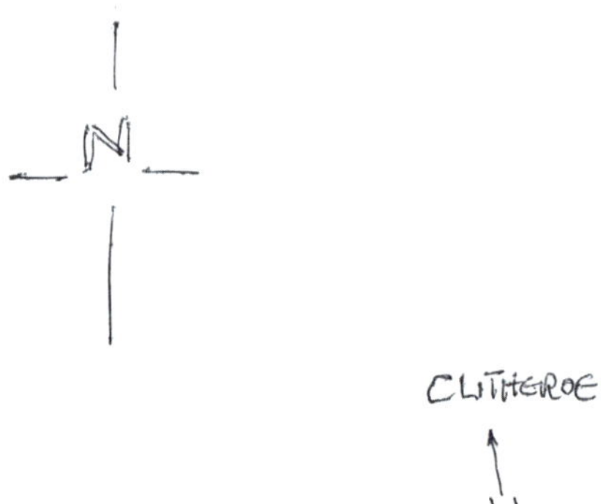

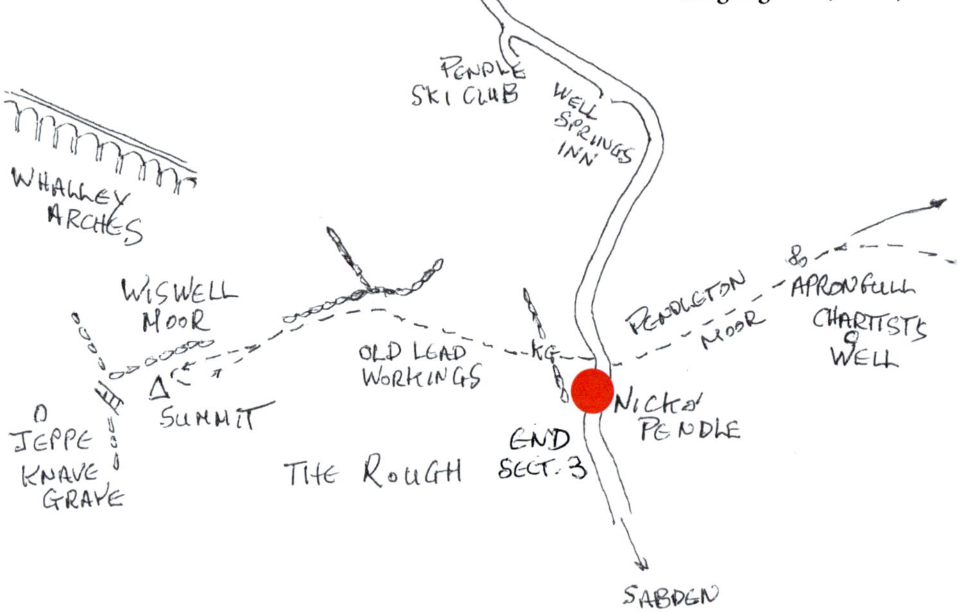

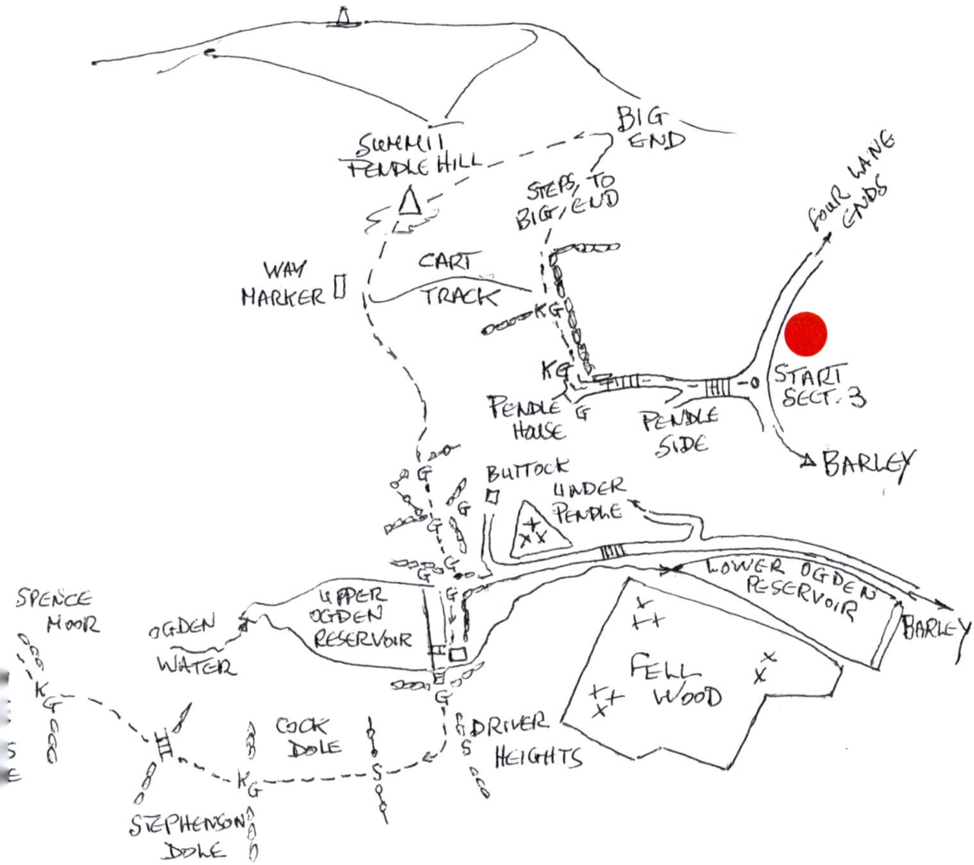

SUMMIT
PENDLE HILL
BIG
END
STEPS, TO
BIG END
FOUR LANE
ENDS
WAY
MARKER
CART
TRACK
KG
KG
START
SECT. 3
PENDLE
HOUSE
G
PENDLE
SIDE
BARLEY
BUTTOCK
UNDER
PENDLE
G
G
G
G
G
LOWER OGDEN
RESERVOIR
BARLEY
SPENCE
MOOR
UPPER
OGDEN
RESERVOIR
OGDEN
WATER
FELL
WOOD
KG
COCK
DOLE
DRIVER
HEIGHTS
S
S
KG
STEPHENSON
DOLE

About this section

This section takes in the last two of the thirteen moors (Spence and Wiswell).

The section starts with the climb up the steps from Pendleside to the Big End, then on to the Trig point and summit of Pendle Hill. Thereafter, follows a descent down the 'Buttock' to Ogden upper reservoir, across the dam, followed by a sharp climb up 'Driver Height' and then right over the top of the Doles and on towards Spence Moor. From Spence moor the route goes around the top of 'Deerstones Cragg', across Badger Wells Water on to Pendleton moor and back to 'The Nick'. The final part of section 3 and the end of the walk takes you across "The Nick' onto Wiswell Moor, the thirteenth and the last moor, where you pass over the area known as the 'Rough' to the trig point, then doubling back to The Nick and the finish.

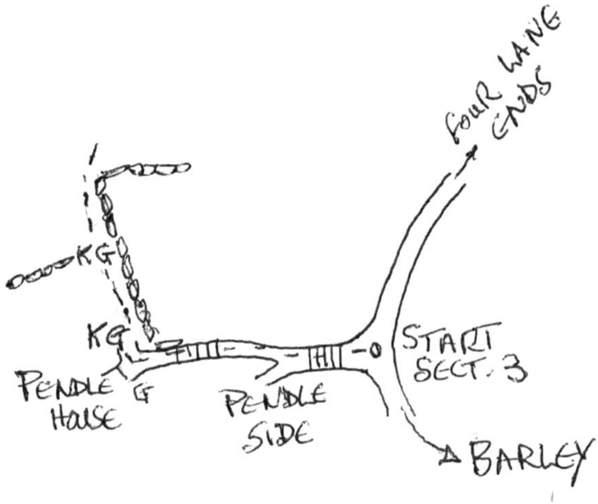

Section 3 starts from Pendleside, where there is roadside parking on Barley Lane

There is no access for vehicles or parking on the farm track to Pendleside

3.1 Farm track towards Pendleside and Pendle House

Follow tarmac track from Barley Lane. When the track forks, keep to right

3.2 Where the track to Pendleside forks, keep right for Pendle and the Big end

> Please note that if you take the left hand fork there is no way through.
>
> You would be met by a dead end and a angry farmer.

Continue along the track

3.3 View on continuation of the track heading for Pendle House

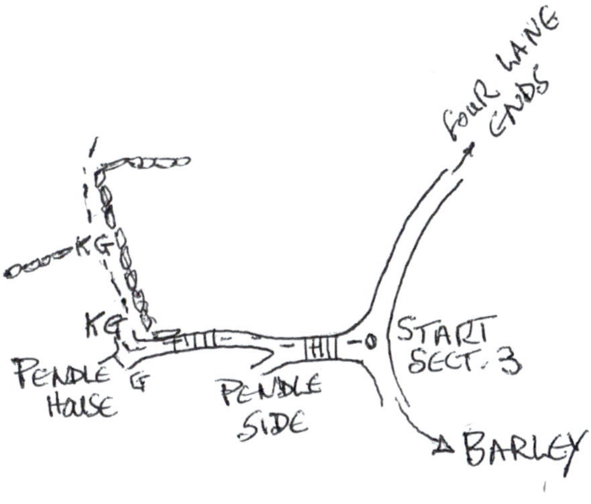

As you approach the two field gates, turn right up a few steps to the kissing gate

3.4 Turn right before Gate to Pendle house to access the fell

> The gate on the left of the picture is private access with no right of way, or through road.
>
> However, just before the gate on the left there is now a pop up snack bar called 'The Cauldron'. Opening times posted on the cabin say Sat & Sun 11.30–4pm, but it also says that these times are not set in tablets of stone.

Pass through the kissing gate and follow the paved path uphill

3.5 Kissing Gate to the fell

On passing through the second kissing gate, take the steps bearing slightly right for the Big End, as this is a more direct and interesting route, due to the extensive views across Ribblesdale, the Yorkshire peaks, and the District of Craven

3.6 Paved path leads to second kissing gate where we bear slightly right and continue up the steps.

> The track to the left is known as the Cart track, and is a more gradual way to the summit, but is often used for the descent, as people feel descending the steps are difficult, and rightly so, particularly when wet or when covered in Snow and Ice.
>
> The Cart track itself gave access onto the summit plateau, but in the main it was used to bring down Millstone Grit (which was, a widely used local building material) from the now overgrown quarry to the left near the top of the track. The paving stones (mill bottoms) used to repair and refurbish the paths on Pendle were reclaimed from demolished mills in and around the area. It's quite possible that some of the paving's could be coming home'!

3.7 Continuation of Steps up the Big End

3.7a The steps in Winter with just a light covering of snow and ice can be difficult to climb without the right gear.

The path gets less steep, as you get closer to the top

3.8 Steps turn to cobbled pavement as you near the top

The steps top out by the stone stile on the Big End (Note: this is the same stile that was traversed towards the end of Section 1 i.e. before the descent of the Big End).

Follow the path round to the left passing the stone cross shelter off to the right before bearing left and heading for the summit trig of Pendle Hill, and crossing Barley Moor for the second time, but in the opposite direction

3.9 The path via the steps tops out by a stone stile

3.10 Black Moss upper and lower reservoirs, as viewed from the Big End, were built between 1894 – 1903 to supply water to Barley and Nelson. However, currently, their water is no longer used for drinking but as 'compensation water' – used to put water back in to the environment.

The reservoirs are stocked with both Brown and Rainbow trout and managed by 'Black Moss Fly Fishing Association'. Day Tickets are available from the 'Barley Picnic site Cabin', or Padiham Angling Centre.

Behind the reservoirs is Aitken wood and sculpture trail. The trail was launched in 2012 for the 400th Anniversary of the Lancashire Witch trials, and added to in 2019.The idea behind the trail came from the artist Phillipe Handford, but more artists contributed, with Phillipe taking the lead. To fund the project, Nelson Town council secured a grant from DEFRA, and United Utilities offered up the use of the woodland. The trail is accessed via a walk from Barley picnic site, along the reservoir road, into the wood, and back. You should allow 3hrs for the 3 mile round trip.

3.11 View left from stone stile to summit, stone shelter is just off to the right

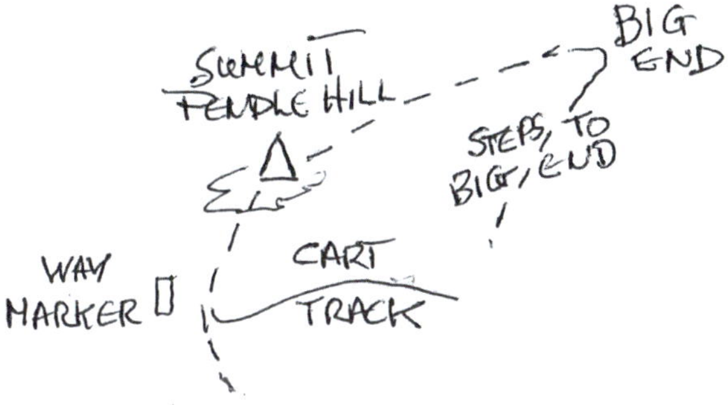

3.12 The shelter is a creative design with the cross being built into, as well as through, the boundary wall.

Built into the RHS wall of the shelter is a stone plaque with the Russian word Kpacota, which when translated seemingly means 'Beauty', or 'pleasing to the eye', which for a drystone Waller, I suppose it definitely is.

It's not known why it was described in Russian

3.13 To the Right of the shelter there is a plaque to George Fox the founder of the Quaker movement.

There is also a drinking Well dedicated to George Fox (Fox's Well), also known as Robin Hoods Well. It's said to be where he paused to quench his thirst on the descent. The Well is accessed down the NNW side of the big end, as mentioned on page 37 of the guide.

3.14 Pendle Hill Trig point with waymarker post and small cairn to the right.

Although standing at 1,827ft (557m) tall, and as such missing out on Mountain status, there is no doubt that its standalone presence dominates the surrounding Landscape.

The Hill has a long history, dating back to the Bronze Age.

In more recent times, the Hill's history became forever intertwined with the infamous Lancashire Witches and the trials of 1612.

Then, on his climb to the summit of the Hill in 1652, George Fox had the 'inspirational vision' that led to the rise of the 'Quaker' movement across England, Ireland and the American colonies.

Less well known was the scientific experiments of Richard Towneley (of Towneley Hall, Burnley), who in 1661 with colleague Henry Powers, conducted his Barometer experiment on the summit, the findings of which, contributed to the discovery of 'Boyle's Law

3.15 Long distance view from the summit, of Black Moss lower reservoir, and edge of Aitken Wood, with the village of Roughlee and its Caravan site in the dip. Roughlee featured in the Witch Hunt of 1612, with Alice Nutter, of Roughlee Hall being wrongfully accused of Witchcraft by a nine year old girl. Unlike others that were accused, Alice never pleaded guilty, but to no avail, as she was hanged along with nine others at Gallows Hill, Lancaster, on 20th August 1612. Those accused of Witchcraft were denied access to Lawyers as well as the right to call witnesses.

3.15a Sculpture (in Roughlee) of 'Alice' (Alice Nutter), by local artist and engineer David Palmer, who sculpted Alice out of Brass and Corten Steel in 2012, to commemorate the 400th anniversary of the infamous witch trials.

3.16 View of Barley Village.

Just over the ridge line at the right of the picture is the village of Newchurch in Pendle, and St Mary's Church. The Church is noted for its 'Eye of God' in the SW face of the Tower that watches over the village. Its said that Alice Nutter was buried here, but its unlikely as Witches were not buried in sacred ground. The village has the 'Witches Galore' shop, well worth a visit for everything Witchy.

3.16a

3.16b

From the trig point, follow the path South heading for a continuation down what is known as 'buttock'

3.17 View S from summit trig, direction Buttock

3.18 Continuation South of track towards Buttock

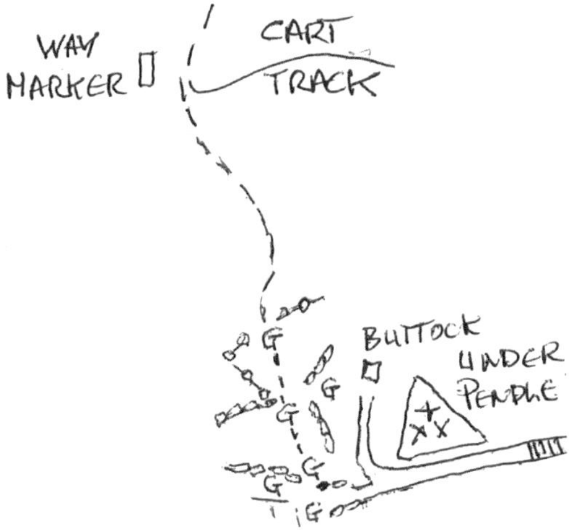

At the junction of paths, take the one straight ahead following the way marker for Pendle Way

3.19 Way marker, direction 'Pendle Way' for Buttock

From the pile of stones at the top of Buttock you can see the route we will follow later across Driver Heights and Spence Moor. For now though we head for the arrow in the centre picture, to the Dam of Upper Ogden Reservoir

3.20 View from the pile of stones at the top of 'Buttock' with the route to the fell gates and Dam marked by the arrow, just off centre of the picture.

To the left is Fell wood, which is the largest of the three plantations that surround the Ogden Reservoirs. It was planted in 1931 with Norway Spruce, Sitka Spruce, Scots Pine and European Larch

3.21 Deep Clough Spring at the top of Buttock

The spring is the start of the drinking water source for the houses at Under Pendle

In all my years of running and walking over here, I have never seen it run dry

Follow the descending path come trod down Buttock to the fell gates and Ogden Clough upper reservoir

3.22 View of rough path and trod down Buttock to Ogden Clough (Lower Ogden reservoir can just be seen on the centre left of the picture).

Ogden Clough reservoirs were built in to supply drinking water to the town of nearby Nelson

When full, the combined upper and lower reservoirs hold upwards of 960,000M3.

The upper reservoir was built in 1906 and the lower in 1914.

The lower reservoir fly fishery was run by the 'Firefly Fishing Club', but unfortunately they have closed the fishery and wound the club up.

3.23 Fell gates at the bottom of Buttock

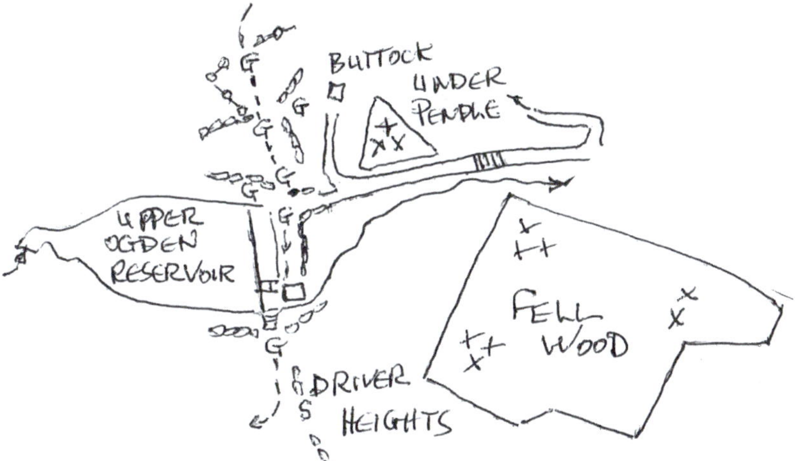

Pass through the wooden, and then the metal gate straight ahead, and descend the field (keeping wall to left) to the gate at the foot of Upper Ogden Dam

3.24 Route through wooden gate and metal gate straight ahead

Farmers continually move livestock around in this area and its important to leave gates as you found them.

3.25 Grass field and trod down to the foot of Ogden Upper reservoir Dam

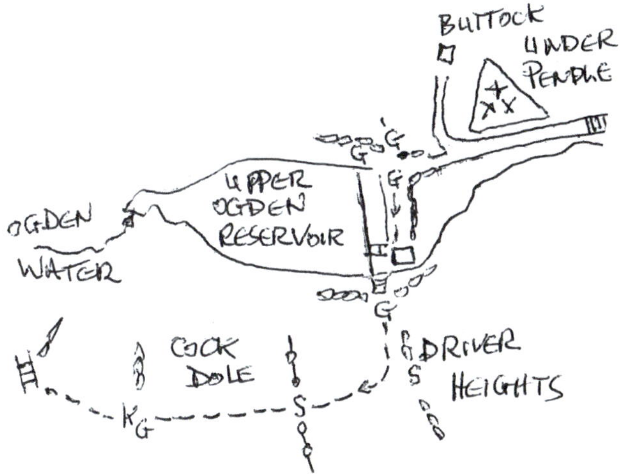

Pass through wooden gate, then Kissing gate, across bottom of Dam and turn right up the steps in the Dam face

3.26 Gate to base of Dam.

To the left of the Dam, the Reservoir Bypass, or Bywash, with its steep descent, is an interesting sight

Climb the steps, turning left at the top

3.27 Steps up the Dam face

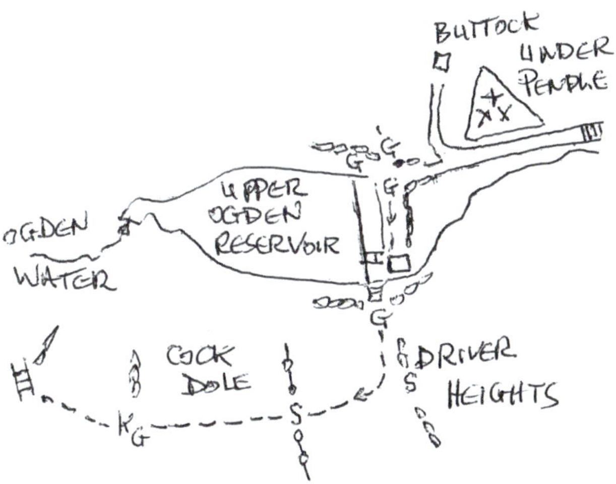

3.28 View from the Top of the Dam to Ogden Lower Reservoir, with Fell Wood to Right and Buttock Wood to the Left.

I'm told by United Utilities that Fell Wood is scheduled for felling due to die back in part of the wood.

3.29 Upper Ogden Reservoir and bypass from the top of the Dam

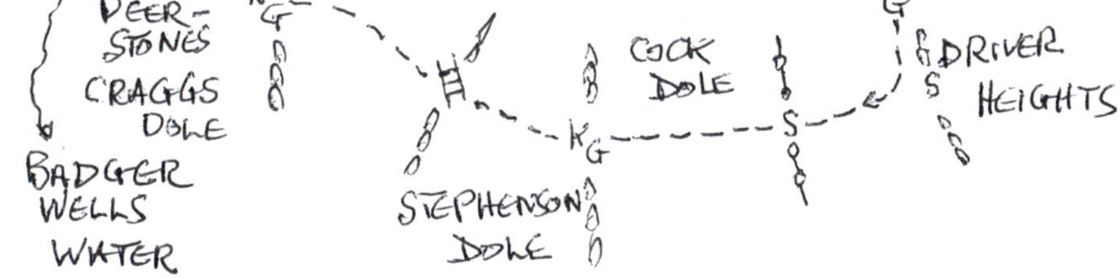

The route continues across the Dam, up the steps to gate and onto the fell. From there, continue up the hill to a junction of paths on Driver Heights.

3.30 View across the top of the dam to the gate leading to the fell and 'Driver heights'

The trod, initially goes straight up, but then drifts closer to the wall and fence on the left as it gets nearer to the top

3.31 View from the gate following a grass trod directly ahead up to Driver Heights

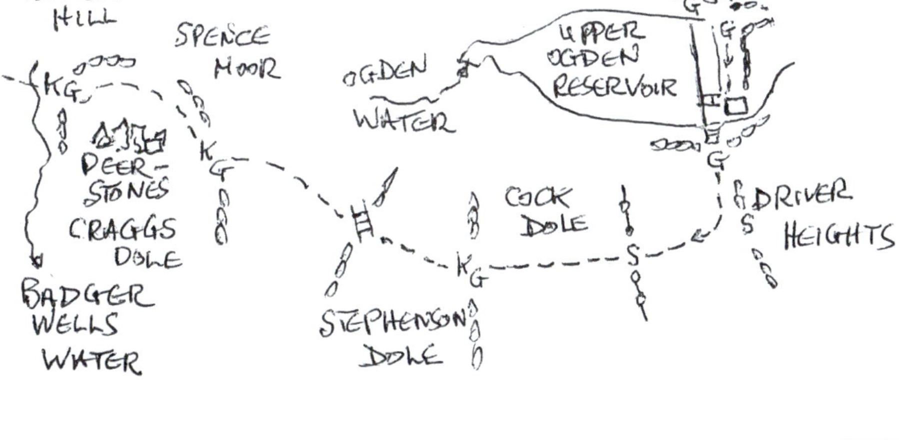

At the junction of the paths turn right, and follow the path trending West in the direction of Spence Moor

3.32 View of junction on Driver Heights. The path you are joining is part of the return route of the annual 'Stan Bradshaw Pendle Round' Fell Race.

The race was named after the local businessman and Fell Running Legend – Stanley Bradshaw. After the war, Stan helped reform Clayton-le-Moors Harriers and later went on to be club president 1959-80. In 1954, Stan ran in the first ever Yorkshire Three Peaks Race, coming second, and with only three out of the six starters finishing. He went on to compete in the race 24 times.

In 1960, Stan became the second person to break the 24hr Bob Graham Round record (comprising 42 peaks over 72 miles and with 28,000ft of ascent). Then in 1977 Stan became the oldest person at 65 to complete the round, a record that stood for 21 yrs., until broken by another Clayton Harrier, 66 year old Brian Leathley.

Continue to follow the path come trod as it starts the gentle ascent up towards Spence Moor

3.33 Path towards Spence Moor

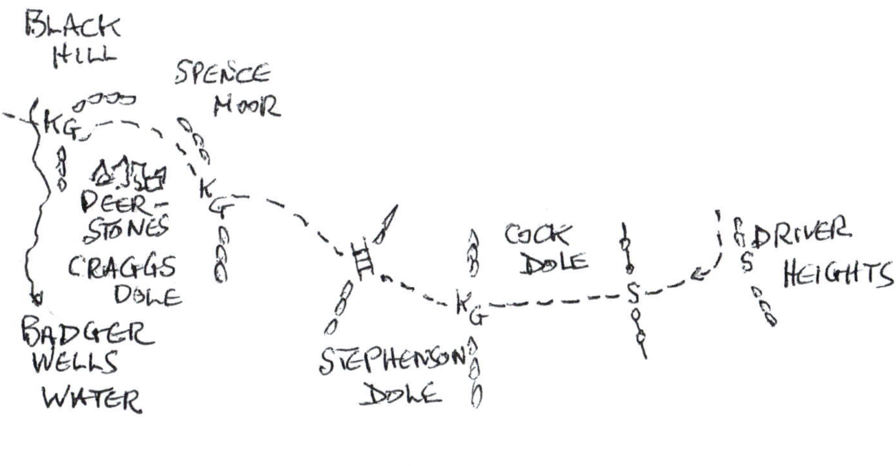

Cross over the stile onto Cock Dole, and follow the path still trending West to a kissing gate heading towards Spence Moor

3.34 Stile on to Cock Dole direction Spence moor.

Of interest, in this area, on either side of the track there are a number of 'Doles' shown on the map – Cock Dole, Lower, Stephenson, Wood House, Stainscomb, and Cragg Dole.

A Dole would have been a small plot of land (part of a bigger Estate, or common land). Each plot would have been marked out by stones, ditches or walls or a combination thereof. Some Doles were given out as common land by goodwill of the Land or Estate owner, others would have been given, or rented to named persons. The Track you are now following, which starts from Hamlet of Sabden fold, would have given cart access to the tops of the Doles as well as relative ease of access between the Doles. This dovetails in to the notes on the 'inclosures' act

Continue along the rising track, aiming just to the right of the wall corner

3.35 Continuation of path to gate in direction of Spence Moor

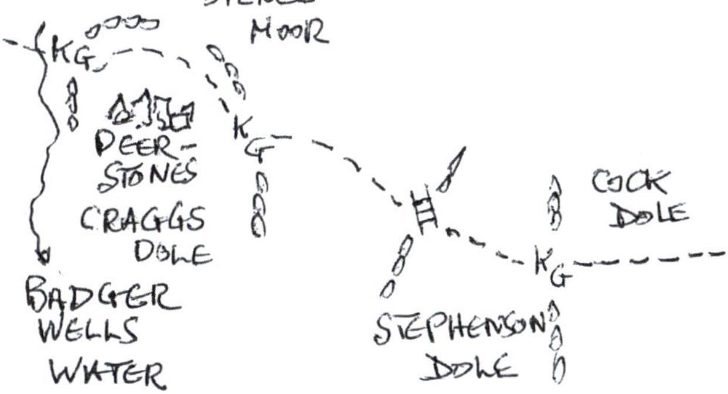

Continue to Kissing gate

3.36 Gate leading onto Stephenson Dole. Through the gate, and on the left is where the Stan Bradshaw Pendle Round would have joined our route, having climbed steeply up Lower Dole from Stainscomb in the valley.

Stan's business by the way was 'Tripe', being an independent processor and supplier from his works in Padiham. As well as Tripe, Bradshaws also offered – Pigs Trotters, Cow heel, Elder (Cow Udder), as well as other less known Offal.

Padiham and other Mill Towns were big consumers, not because it was particularly nutritious or tasty, but rather because it was relatively cheap.

I liked lashings of malt Vinegar on my Tripe and Elder!

Pass through the gate and still trending West, climb on an indistinct path come trod, the very wet and boggy Stephenson Dole, heading for a ladder stile onto Spence Moor, shown by the arrow in the middle of the skyline

3.37 View through gate across Stephenson Dole to a ladder stile on the skyline

3.38 Stile to top of Spence Moor

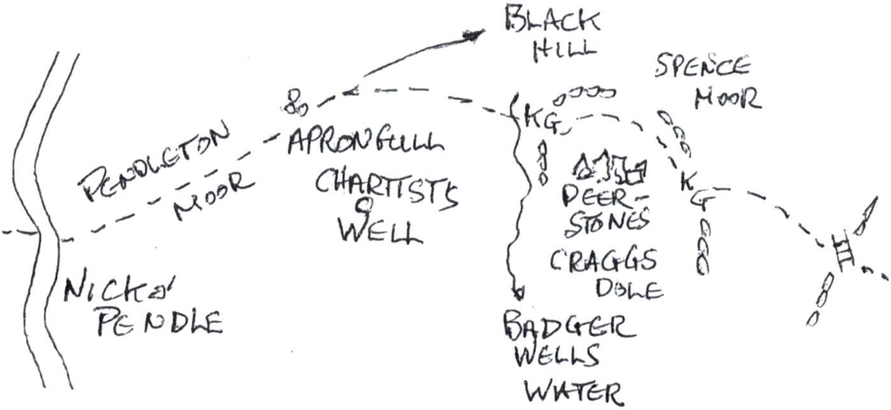

Climb over the stile and follow the path come trod to the left, which soon curves around to the right heading for a kissing gate, direction Craggs Dole and Deerstones.

3.39 View over stile onto Spence Moor with path to left

Follow path heading for a Kissing Gate, shown by the arrow on the centre skyline

3.40 Continuation of path across Spence Moor towards Kissing Gate

Pass through the gate and turn right

3.41 Gate onto top of Craggs Dole and Deerstones

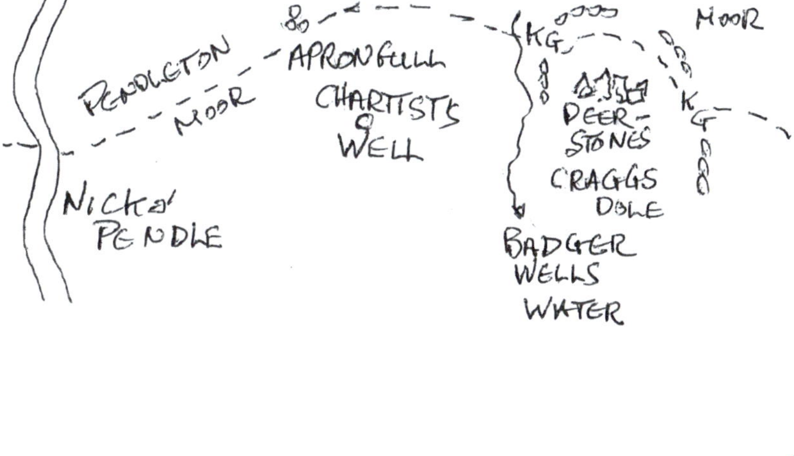

Having passed through the gate and turned right follow a trod and keep the wall to your right

Do not attempt to approach Deerstones from the top side as the crag face is a sheer drop off

3.42 View over the gate with the path to right

Continue along the route keeping the wall a few yards to your right

3.43 View of route along the top of Craggs Dole and Deerstones

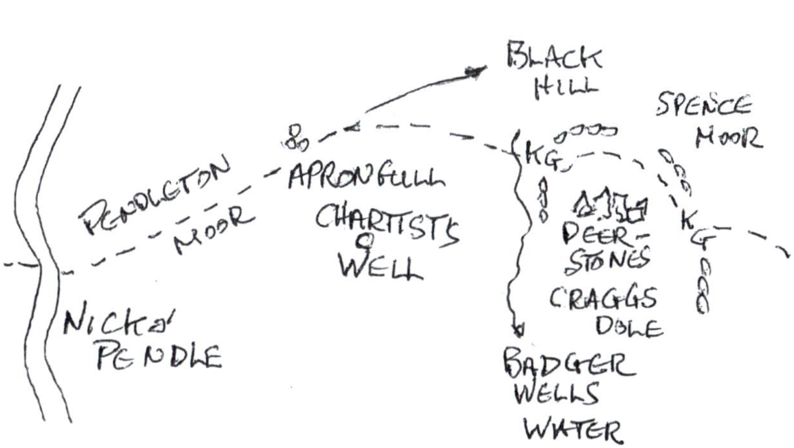

The track and wall bear to the left (trending South) and descend to a Kissing gate on the right, which leads on to Badger Wells

3.44 Continuation of path towards Badger Wells, Pendleton Moor and Apronfull

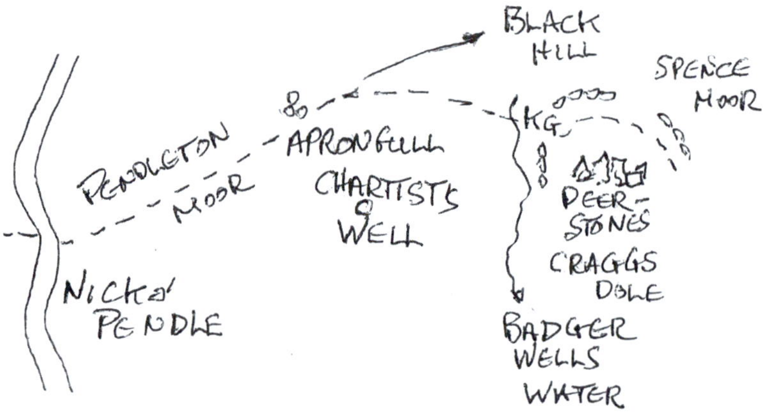

Pass through the gate crossing Badger Wells water and back on to Pendleton Moor and Apronfull

3.45 Kissing gate onto Pendleton Moor crossing over Badger Wells Water

Continue straight ahead, on the track come trod, eventually bearing left to join the track trending Southwest to the top of Apronfull

3.46 Path across Badger Wells to Apronfull

Descend Apronfull and continue back towards the Nick

3.47 View from Badger Wells to the top of Apronfull, with Wiswell Moor in the far distance

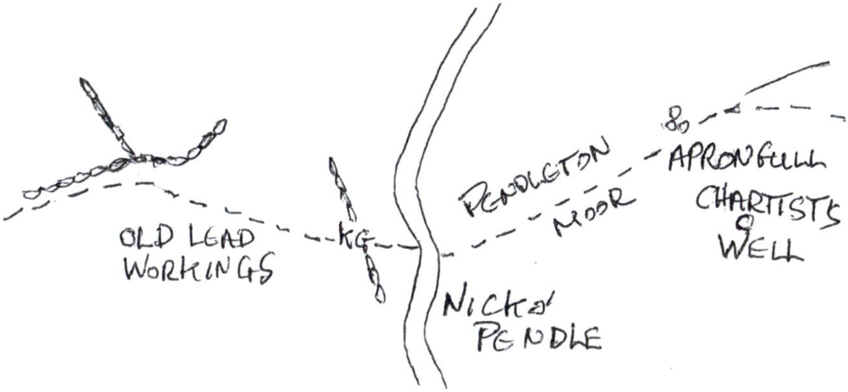

Continue with the descent of Apronfull

3.48 View of the Nick and Wiswell Moor from Apronfull

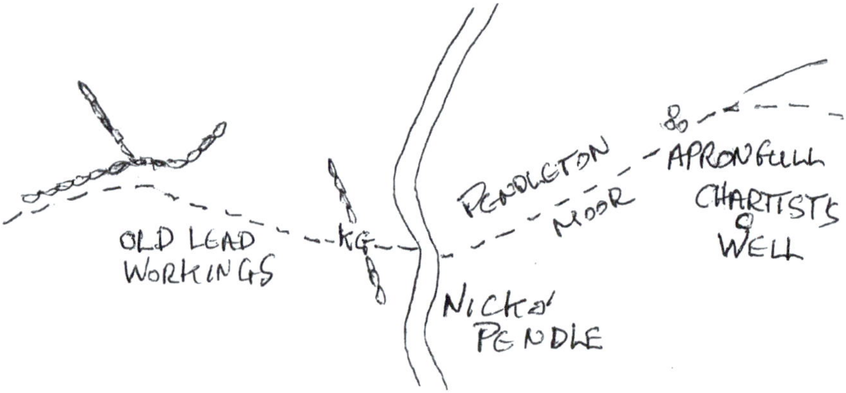

3.49 View to left (south east) of Churn Clough Reservoir from Apronfull.

Churn Clough was built in the late 1800's and extended (to 16 acres) in the 1920's to meet the ever growing need for water in the in the nearby, small town, of Padiham.

The need was due to the fact that at its peak (circa 1900), there were 22 Mills running, with over 11,000 looms employed in the manufacture of cotton.

On the back of such a high number of Mills and growing population, came the development of necessary support industries such as Engineering, Foundry work and Bobbin manufacture.

Churn Clough is regularly stocked with Brown and Rainbow trout from the Dunsop Bridge Fishery, and is run by Colne Water Angling Club. Day permits are available from Padiham Angling Centre, or the 'Lakeside café' in Colne

Arrival back at the Nick

3.50 looking across Nick o' Pendle to Wiswell – the thirteenth and final moor

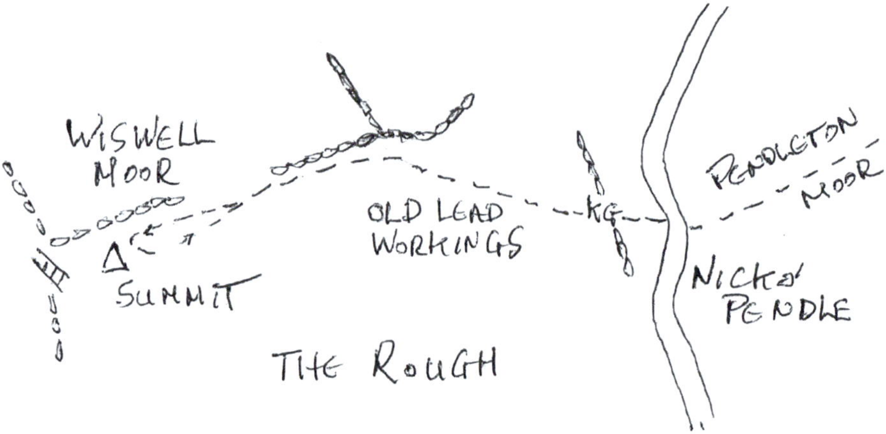

Crossover the Nick to the West side, clambering up the exposed rock slabs of the disused quarry, or the green path to the side. Then head towards a kissing gate leading onto Wiswell Moor for the last leg of Section 3 and the walk

3.51 Nick o' Pendle

Pass through the kissing gate on to Wiswell Moor and follow the path across the area known as the 'Rough' to where it merges with the wall on the left

3.52 Kissing gate leading to Wiswell Moor.

> The name 'Rough', given to this part of the moor is thought to be derived from the fact that the land, being boggy and reed covered, was only fit for 'rough grazing' of Hill Sheep and Cattle

Continue on the track heading for the walls in the distance

3.53 Track across moor towards the Trig

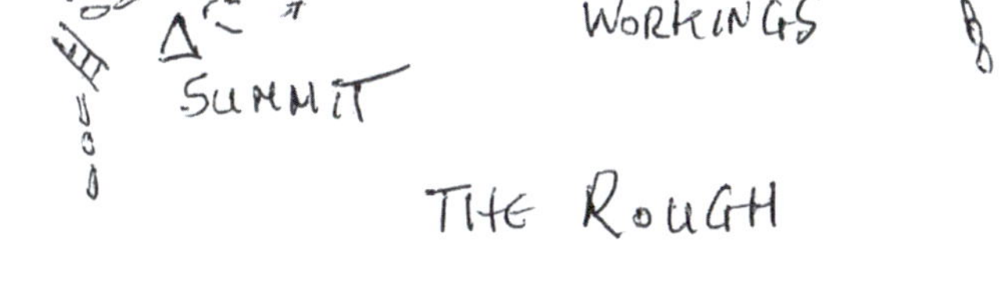

Continue along the track, which can be boggy on this section

3.54 Continuation of track, heading towards the wall in the dip

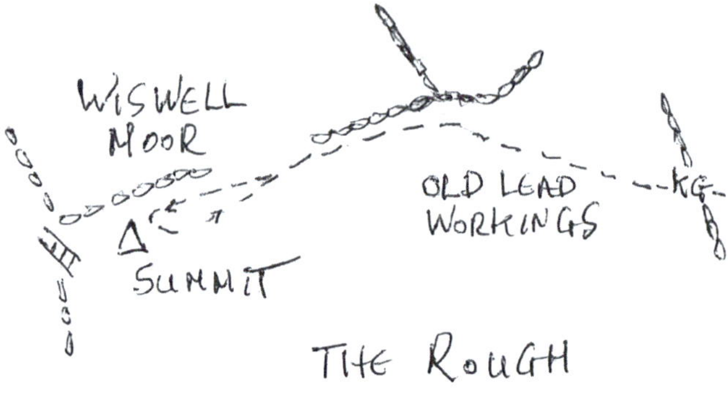

Continue on towards dip in the track keeping wall to the right

3.55 Continuation of rough track

At the junction of paths, take the grass path uphill, to the right, and keeping the wall to your right

3.56 Continuation of path towards the Trig point.

This area and the surroundings were the site of open cast lead mining. Whilst further down the slope to the left (south east), just off the track between Paslew Barn and Wilkin Heys are what appears to be the remains of an open, vertical shaft mine.

However, without a water source nearby and any visible evidence of industrialisation, it's thought that the work here would have been small scale and as such the ore would have been taken elsewhere for processing

Track continues uphill across the moor towards the trig

3.57 Continuation of track across the moor keeping wall to the right

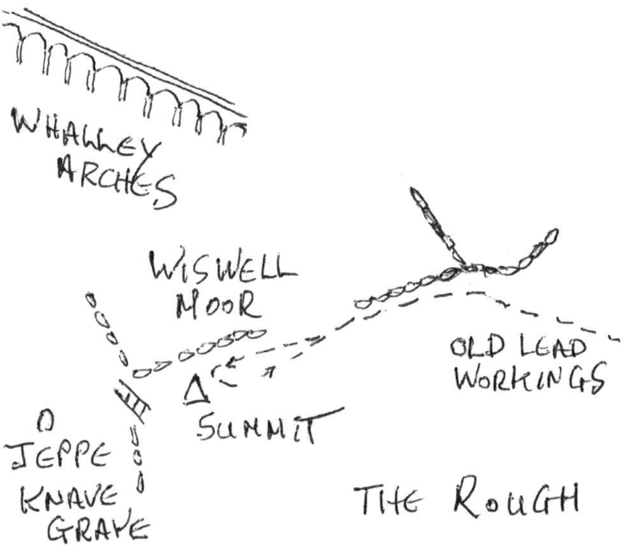

Continuation of track with Trig point now in view

3.58 Path to trig point on the skyline

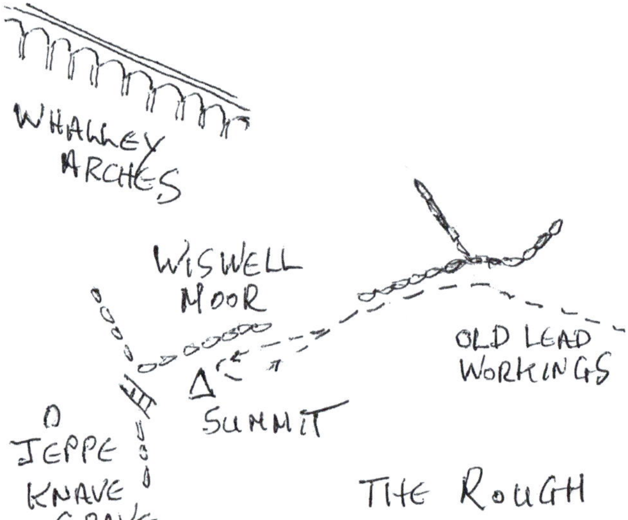

3.59 View from the moor to the village of Pendleton, with Clitheroe in the background

3.59a The village of Pendleton with Wiswell Moor behind

3.60 Summit of Wiswell Moor at 1,037ft (316m)

Unfortunately you cannot see the village of Wiswell from the summit, as it's below the tree line in the middle distance

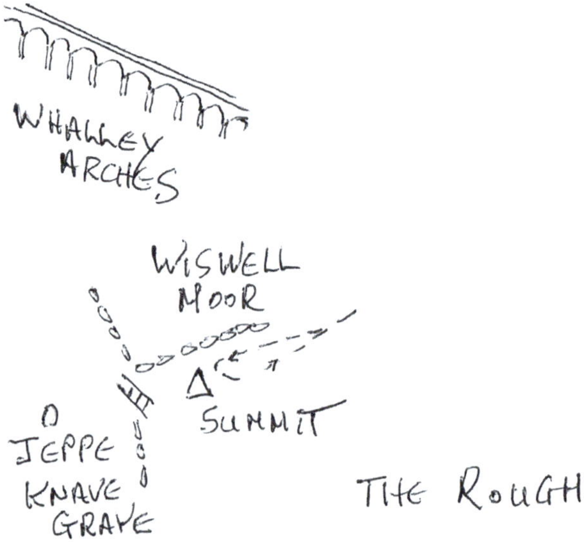

3.61 View south west from Trig of; L-R Whalley Nab, Billington, Whalley Viaduct, and Whalley

A landmark of the area is the 600m long Whalley Viaduct, known locally as the 'Whalley Arches'.

The Arches which cross the River Calder were finished in 1850, having been constructed from 12,000m3 of stone and 7 million bricks, made locally at the time, by the George Clarke Brickworks, Rishton. The Viaduct has 49 arches, more than double that of the more famous Ribblehead Viaduct, with 24.

The line runs freight and some special steam heritage trips, but there is a campaign to have it re opened for scheduled passenger and Tourism services which would allow them to connect directly with the Settle-Carlisle line.

3.61a Same view, but this time looking towards a wall corner with a gate and stile marked by the arrow.

If you were to go through the gate then climb over the Ladder stile and follow the descending path for about 150yds, you would come to what is known as 'Jeppe Knave Grave', which is not part of the route, but you may, in any case, wish to visit it.

On the subject of Jeppe Knave, you could write a good few pages, however, I try to summarise the more popular stories and beliefs, whilst leaving food for thought.

The gravestone sits to the edge of what is said to have been a chambered Neolithic or Bronze Age burial site. The site is well noted, but there are no records of it ever having been excavated, and if you compare my 2023 photographs of the site to older ones that have been published over the years, you can see that the gravestone has been moved around, so you would in any case be unsure of where to scan and dig for Jeppe's remains.

361b Burial site (looking back to the Trig), with grave stone to right hand side

3.61c The name on the gravestone is barely visible

Jeppe or Jeffry Curtis or Curteys was said to be either an outlaw of the hunting grounds, or a highwayman of the region, somewhere during the period 11th to 14th Century's.

The origins of the name Knave can be related to someone of common or low breeding, a wrongdoer or maybe a servant.

The death of Jeppe is unclear, but it is thought that he was either captured and beheaded, or ambushed and killed.

As for the burial, it's hard to believe that you would go to all the trouble of getting the body onto the high moor to bury it, however, the ancient burial site, could be seen as Pagan and as such linked to the devil. That being the case, then it could be seen as a suitable site to bury a wrongdoer.

Continuing with the route – retrace your steps back to the Nick

3.62, 3.62a & b Heading back to the Nick, with long views L–R of Mearley, Apronfull, Black Hill behind, and Deerstones Crag to the right

Deerstones Crag is part of folklore, because at its base, amongst thousands of boulders, are the 'Devils, or Giants Footprints'. It's said that the Devil, or 'Owd Nick', leapt over to Pendle from nearby Hameldon hill (see inset picture viewed from the footprints), to fill his apron with stones, and in doing saw left his footprints. Loaded with stones, the Devil then crossed to Apronfull and began throwing them at Clitheroe, making the hole in the side of the castle keep.

3.63a View from 'The Rough' looking to the left towards the Wellsprings bar and restaurant and the Pendle Ski Club.

Mearley and Apronfull in the back ground.

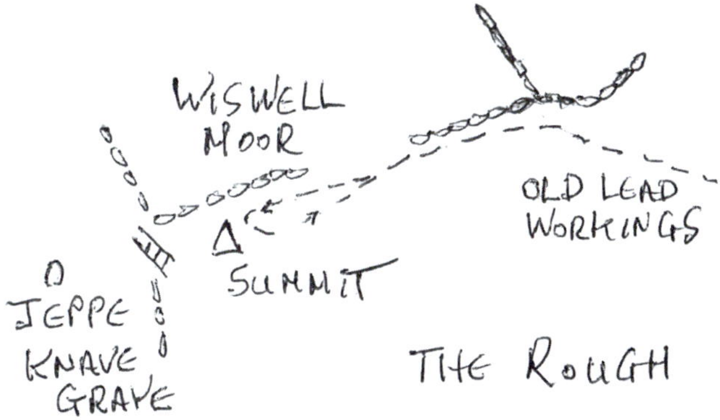

3.63 View from 'The Rough' looking to the right, towards the village of Sabden

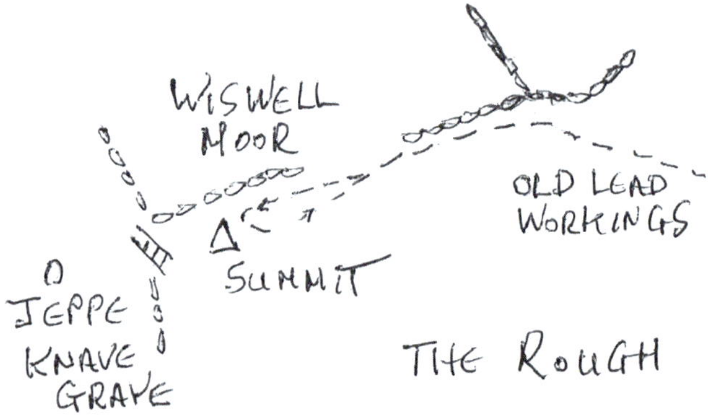

3.64 Finally you're back where you started, and the end of the Coven of 13 Moors walk

Congratulations, well done. I hope you had good clear weather and enjoyed it

You have just walked over 17 miles and climbed 3,260ft (which is more than England's highest Mountain – Scafell Pike at 3,209ft). You have also traversed 13 moors and hopefully taken in some great views, landscapes, wildlife, and Historical notes

Index to the guide

	Section
17th century cottage	1&2
Air crash Memorial	1
Aitken Family	2
Aitken Wood	3
Alice Nutter	3
Annel Cross	2
Apronfull	1&3
Armstrong, Duncan	2
Army and Tank training WW2	1
Ashdean Clough	1
Badger Wells	1&3
Badger Wells Water	3
Barley Lane	1, 2 & 3
Barley Moor	1&3
Barley Mow	Intro & 2
Barley Picnic site and Village	2
Battle of Preston	1
Big End	1,2 & 3
Billington	3
Black Hill	1 & 2
Black Moss Farm	2
Black Moss Fly Fishing Association	3
Black Moss Reservoirs	2
Black Moss Road	2
Blacko Tower	2
Bollard Family	2
Bollard Wood	2
Boothman Park	2
Bowland Fells	1
Bronze Age Burial Mound	1
Burnley Football Club (BFC)	2
Buttock	3
Camp School	2
Cart or Pony Track	3

	Section
Chartists	1
Churn Clough Reservoir	3
Clayton-Le-Moors Harriers Memorial Cairn	1
Clitheroe Castle	1
Clitheroe Cement Works	1
Clitheroe Road	1 & 3
Colne	3
Colne Water	2
Colne Water Angling Club	3
Coolham Farm	2
Deerstones	3
DEFRA	3
Devil's Apronful	1
Dole	3
Downham	1
Downham Moor	1
Driver Height	3
Eye of God	3
Fell Wood	3
Firefly Fishing Club	3
Foot House Gate	2
Four Lane Ends Milestone	2
Fountains Fell	2
Four Lane ends	2
Fox's Well	3
Gallows Hill	3
George Fox & the Quaker Movement	3
Giants Footprints	1
Gragareth	2
Hameldon Hill	3
Helliwell Wood	2
Higher Black Moss	2
Higher Black Moss Reservoir	2
Higher Twiston	2
Ing Head Moor	1
Ingleborough	2
Jeppe Knave Grave	3

	Section
Kenneth Oldham	2
Kpacota	3
Longridge Fell	1
Lower Black Moss Reservoir	1
Lead Mining	3
Little Mearley Hall	1
Lower Black Moss	2
Lower Black Moss Reservoir	2
Lower Ogden Reservoir	2
Malkin Tower	2
Mearley	3
Mearly Moor	1
Mill Bottoms	3
Mountain Farm	2
Narrowgates, Narrowgates Mill & Cottages	2
Newchurch in Pendle	3
Nick o' Pendle	1 & 3
Occupation Lane	2
Ogden Clough	1
Ogden Clough Reservoirs	3
Oliver Cromwell	1
Overhouses	2
Padiham	3
Padiham Angling Centre	3
Paslew Barn	3
Pendle Inn	Intro & 2
Pendle Moor	1
Pendleside	2 & 3
Pendleton Moor	1 & 3
Pendle Summit	1 & 3
Pendle Water	2
Pennine Way	2
Pen-y-ghent	2
Pike Law	1
Quaker Movement	1
Reef Knoll	1
Richard Towneley	3

	Section
Rimmington	1 & 2
Rimmington Moor	2
Roughlee and Roughlee Hall	3
Sabden	Intro
Sawley Abbey	1
Scout Cairn	1
Sculpture Trail	3
Shelter Cairn	1
Shelter cross, Big End	1
Smithy Fold	2
South Lakeland Fells	1
Spence Moor	3
Stang	2
Stang Top	2
Stang Top Road	2
Steps up Big End	3
St Mary's Church	3
The Cabin	Intro & 2
The Rough	3
The Wellsprings	Intro
Towneley Hall	3
Twiston Moor	2
United Utilities	2 & 3
Upper Ogden Reservoir and Dam	3
Walverden Water	2
Whalley	3
Whalley Nab	3
Whalley Viaduct or Whalley Arches	3
Whernside	2
Whitehough	2
Whitehough Camp School	2
White Hough Water	2
Wilkin Heys	3
Windy Harbour	2
Wiswell Moor	3
Witches Altar	2
Witches Coven	2

	Section
Witches Galore	3
Worsaw Hill	1
Worston	1
Worston Boundary Stone	1
Worston Moor	1
Yorkshire Peaks	1 & 2

Maps to accompany the Guide Book

[1] OS Explorer OL41 – FOREST OF BOWLAND & RIBBLESDALE Pendle Hill, Clitheroe & Settle

(This map, with the exception of the West side of Wiswell Moor and the trig, covers the complete route of the guide)

[2] OS Explorer 287 – WEST PENNINE MOORS
Blackburn, Darwen, Accrington & Bolto North

(This map is only required for the last couple of miles of the route – Wiswell Moor, end of section 3, the last section of the guide)

[3] OS Landranger 103 – BLACKBURN & BURNLEY
Clitheroe & Skipton

(This map covers the complete route, but lacks detail as it is only 1:50 000 scale – it's OK for an overview)

[4] Armstrong, Duncan., & Associates., ed (circa 1996/97) Paths Around PENDLE Hurst Green, Hodder Bridges & Whalley Nab. A detailed footpath and visitor Map. Padiham: Armstrong

(This double sided map based on OS maps up to 1932, the front side of the map covers the complete guide route)

The map is currently out of print, but after face to face discussion with Duncan Armstrong himself, it seems that actions are ongoing to see if there could be a reprint

Sources of information

Unless specifically mentioned otherwise, all the information and historical notes in the guide are from open sources, common 'local' knowledge/folklore, or word of mouth.